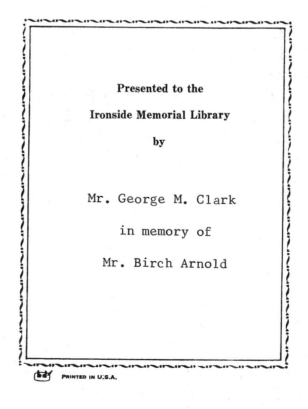

The
CONSTITUTION
of the
UNITED STATES

The CONSTITUTION of
OUR CHARTER OF LIBERTIES

We the People

the UNITED STATES

by JAMES MUSSATTI

D. VAN NOSTRAND COMPANY, INC.

PRINCETON, NEW JERSEY

TORONTO   LONDON

NEW YORK

D. VAN NOSTRAND COMPANY, INC.
120 Alexander St., Princeton, New Jersey (*Principal office*)
24 West 40 Street, New York 18, New York

D. VAN NOSTRAND COMPANY, LTD.
358, Kensington High Street, London, W.14, England

D. VAN NOSTRAND COMPANY (Canada), LTD.
25 Hollinger Road, Toronto 16, Canada

Published simultaneously in Canada by
D. VAN NOSTRAND COMPANY (Canada), LTD.

Library of Congress Catalogue Card No. 60–12088

Illustrations by Paul Orban

10664a30
PRINTED IN THE UNITED STATES OF AMERICA

Preface

THE CONSTITUTION OF THE UNITED STATES—OUR CHARTER OF LIBERTIES will increase your understanding of the meaning and importance of the Constitution of the United States.

The pageant of events and movements leading to the formation and expression of the basic principles of this nation's government is unfolded step by step. The struggle of the English barons and clergy to secure the recognition of their rights by the king, the persistence of the early American colonists to preserve their rights as Englishmen, our defense of the freedoms we possess as citizens of the United States—all these acts are seen as being related. It is clearly outlined how the beliefs and actions of peoples past and present have influenced the framework of government under which we live.

The Constitution of the United States is examined article by article and section by section. The meaning and scope of its various provisions and the amendments to it are explained. At the same time the historical background of the amendments is given so that the reader can appreciate the reasons for their adoption at a particular time in the history of this country. He will view the drama and the trials behind the Constitution, from its ratification to the current controversy over the interpretation of civil and state's rights.

The material presented in this book is of interest to all those living under the Constitution. Therefore, the author has made a special effort to employ a style of writing that will appeal to the widest possible audience. The treatment found herein is neither technical nor learned. Of necessity, much basic historical and legal material had to be omitted because of lack of space and the desire to keep the narrative focused on the fundamental principles of the Constitution.

The author hopes that this short and straightforward story of the Constitution will be of help in bringing alive the desires and aspirations of those who wrote and developed this document and that it will deepen the reader's appreciation of the struggles for freedom undertaken by earlier generations.

JAMES MUSSATTI

San Francisco, California
April, 1960

Acknowledgments

This book is the result of the encouragement and stimulus of many people.

I wish first to express my indebtedness to Mrs. A. C. Mattei and Mr. Herbert W. Clark, and to American Principle, Inc., for permission to appropriate here portions of *Constitutionism* which I wrote for them in 1941. They have always encouraged me to continue my interest in the Constitution.

Secondly, I wish to acknowledge my debt to Dr. L. T. Lowrey, President of Blue Mountain College, for imparting to me an understanding and an appreciation of the American Constitution and of American history.

Thanks go to my brother, Anthony, for careful review of the manuscript and for the indexing of the volume.

Helpful suggestions were made by my son David and by my secretaries, Mrs. Carol A. Hickman and Miss Evelyn Rudolph. For the job of typing the manuscript I must thank Miss Nancy Cope and Miss Ruth Westerland.

Finally, without the inspiration, patience, and understanding of my wife, there would have been no book.

J. M.

Contents

The
CONSTITUTION
of the
UNITED STATES

We the People of the United States in order to form a more perfect Union establish Justice insure domestic Tranquility provide for the common defence promote the general Welfare and secure the Blessings of Liberty to ourselves and do ordain and establish this Constitution

Article 1

Section 1. All legislative Powers herein granted shall be vested in a Congress of the United States

CHAPTER 1

The English Background

For thousands of years before the turn of the eighteenth century, mankind had failed to construct a stable and long-lasting government that could provide individual freedom and opportunity. Experiments in the art of governing had run the gamut from mob rule to one-man dictatorship: democracy, autocracy, and monarchy—in all their various forms and manifestations—had been tried. Of all these attempts at government, none could guarantee life, liberty, and the pursuit of happiness to the succeeding generations of men living under them. Instead, each eventually brought misery, chaos, and oppression. Each fell into a tyranny of persecution and military despotism, ending in the ruination of the ideals and prosperity of man. In no phase of the cycle of experiments in government could the rights of the individual be secured.

Fortunately, the forefathers of this great nation came into the pages of history with the wisdom and the ability required to profit from the sad experiences of mankind. It was not by accident that WE, the people of the United States, live under a Constitution dedicated to the preservation of the "rights of man." How these pioneers in America, faced with almost insurmountable hardships and opposition, were able to mold a free government dedicated to the protection of the public welfare is *one of the soul-stirring epics of mankind.* That great epic is part of the story of this book.

Magna Carta

The drafters of our Constitution understood those lessons of English history which taught in dramatic episodes the possibility of oppression through misrule of kings. The story begins with a bit of parchment called the Magna Carta. Behind it lies the long

2

and bitter history of a relentless struggle by generations of Englishmen against the tyranny of their rulers. In it is the basis of American liberty. At the point of the sword, in the meadow at Runnymede on a little island in the River Thames, King John of England was forced to sign the Magna Carta. He had oppressed his people and had ruled arbitrarily. He had trampled upon the "ancient rights of Englishmen." The entire nation had suffered from John's misrule. Yet the threat of cold steel at Runnymede on June 15, 1215, sufficiently convinced him that limiting his powers with the pen was far more desirable than limiting his existence by the sword.

The king was compelled to rule under the provisions of law and no longer by the whims of his fancies. Thus was the principle of limited monarchy established in England. Law was made supreme over the realm by the Magna Carta. It was recognized that the king was no longer the sole source of civil law.

The importance of the Magna Carta in the history of our liberty lies in the fact that it provided *the restraint of written law*. The rights of Englishmen were specified in writing. The Great Charter set them forth one by one, clearly and emphatically. No one was to be denied justice. No one was to be imprisoned or dispossessed of his property or rights except according to the law or the "judgment of his peers." The present right of Americans to a trial by jury and their

right to appeal to a court of law when threatened with dispossession of any personal or property rights are first expressed in the Magna Carta. Extraordinary taxes could not be levied except with the consent of the representatives of the people. In this we find the forerunner of the slogan of the American Revolution, "no taxation without representation."

Four Fundamental Principles

Important to the subsequent history of the world, the Magna Carta established in written form four fundamental principles. First, the king must rule in accordance with the desires of the people. Second, government is a contract between the king and the people that neither one can break without being called to account. Third, the arbitrary power of the king is limited by many restrictions contained in the charter. Fourth, the rights of Englishmen are stated definitely and exactly.

Petition of Right

Four hundred years passed over the meadowlands of Runnymede and over the dust of King John and his nobles. The people of England were in a state of unhappiness and oppression, for once again their king wilfully disregarded Englishmen's rights and privileges. Their property was confiscated without the process

4

William R.   Mary

of law. They were imprisoned on command of the king without
trial by jury. Soldiers were boarded in their homes without their
consent. Government was carried on without the representatives
of the people. Boldly they set out to reassert the rights and principles of the Magna Carta, now utterly disregarded by King
Charles I. Thus, in 1628 Parliament flatly refused to vote any
money for the operation and maintenance of the kingdom unless
Charles restored those rights. So, on June 7, 1628, not at the point
of the sword, but by control of the "purse strings" through law,
Charles I was forced to sign the Petition of Right.

Here again were laid down four fundamental principles of
government. First, all taxes are to be levied only with the consent
of Parliament. Second, troops are not to be boarded in private
homes without the owners' consent. Third, martial law cannot
be declared in time of peace. Fourth, every person is entitled to
trial by jury and "judgment by his peers," and no arbitrary im-
prisonments are to be made. These four principles are embodied
in the Constitution of the United States. Without them, the individual could not enjoy personal security.

Reaffirmation of Principles

Arbitrary dissolution of Parliament and the continued violation
of these rights brought Charles I to the headman's block in 1649.

The monarchy was not restored until 1660, when Charles II swore allegiance to the principles of the Magna Carta and the Petition of Right.

For 28 years after the coronation of Charles II in 1660, the now-traditional rights of Englishmen were preserved. But again a king ruled who denied any responsibility to the people. The belief of James II in absolute monarchy brought about his abdication and the Revolution of 1688, which permanently established the power of Parliament and the right of the people to govern England. Declaring the throne vacant, Parliament elected William and Mary as rulers, and in 1689 they approved the Bill of Rights. Never again in the history of England were the inalienable rights of Englishmen ever questioned by a monarch.

Bill of Rights

Political liberty had triumphed in England. The Bill of Rights asserted the people's right to petition for a redress of their grievances. It declared excessive bail and fines as well as cruel and unusual punishments to be illegal. The right of the people to bear arms was established. It provided that taxes could not be levied except by Parliament. Free elections and frequent meetings of Parliament were affirmed as necessary to the preservation of the laws. It denied that the king had the right to suspend laws or create courts or commissions outside the law. It proclaimed freedom of speech in Parliamentary debates. The profound significance and value to Americans of these early fundamentals of government is easily realized, for *in the first eight amendments to the Constitution of the United States we find the influence of the Petition of Right and the Bill of Rights.*

During the occurrence of these events in England, Englishmen who were too impatient to await the hour of victory were slowly migrating to America to escape religious and political persecution. Rather than submit to the requirements of a king's political and religious prejudices, the founders of America chose to follow the dictates of their consciences by facing the sacrifice, privation, and suffering necessary in conquering a wilderness and in becoming men of freedom in America.

Three Advocates of Liberty

The founding fathers of the Constitution were thoroughly familiar with the Magna Carta, the Petition of Right, the Bill of Rights, and the dark hours in the history of liberty which brought forth these immortal documents. In addition, they were familiar with the ideas of many learned men who had written of mankind's struggle for liberty. Chief among these were two Englishmen, John Locke and Sir William Blackstone, and a Frenchman, Baron de Montesquieu.

John Locke, the son of a Puritan soldier, was the philosopher of the Whig party. Every leader of the American Revolution, in arguing for American independence and the natural rights of man, quoted his clearly reasoned philosophies from his *Treatises of Government,* published in 1690.

Natural Rights

According to this philosopher, the natural rights of man consist of life, liberty, and property. He regarded maintenance of life as the basis of all human existence, with natural law giving man the right to do any reasonable thing to preserve it. Thus, liberty is freedom from every rule except the law of nature. Property is the right under natural law to control the objects necessary to the preservation of life. Whenever a man introduces his own labor into any such object, it becomes his private property to use, to trade, or to give away.

In order to protect and preserve life, liberty, and property, Locke claimed that man forms a political community by "social contract." According to the theory of "social contract," men voluntarily agree to restrict their rights and liberty to carry out the laws of nature by entering into union with other men. The laws of nature are enforced through the formation of a political society which will determine a uniform interpretation of these laws, thereby establishing the rights of life, liberty and property. As an impartial agency, the government must apply this interpretation between individual members of society. Locke regarded government without written law as arbitrary and contrary to the laws of nature.

In order to achieve the protection of man's natural rights, Locke believed that the legislative branch of government should be supreme. However, the existence not only of legislative power but also of executive or administrative power was recognized as necessary. He considered four limitations upon the legislative branch as imperative to achieve good government. First, the legislature cannot be arbitrary. It must rule according to the laws of nature. Second, the legislature must not transgress the written laws. Third, the legislature cannot take from any man any of his property without that man's consent. And fourth, the legislature under no circumstances can transfer to any other agency its power to make laws.

The right to life, liberty, and property could not be legitimately denied by government, as Locke had pointed out. Was not this the sole and only purpose for the existence of government? *The state was the servant of the individual and not the individual the servant of the state.* Liberty, to the belief of the American of 1776, was a God-given right. No power—economic or political—could shatter that belief. With the United States Constitution, our founders hoped to promote the general welfare in keeping with the philosophy of Locke in natural rights. Hence, the scope of activity and authority of government over the individual was carefully defined and restricted.

Separation of Powers

There was published in France in 1748 a book entitled *Spirit of the Laws,* the author of which was a former French magistrate named Montesquieu. He believed that liberty could exist only when the power of the government was limited. This he found to be the case under the English form of government, and therefore, he approved of the English system. He gave to the world the doctrine of the separation of powers, the preservation of liberty by dividing government into three great departments: executive, legislative, and judicial. The framers of our Constitution believed firmly with Montesquieu that: "When the legislative and executive powers are united in the same person, or in the same body of magistrates, there can be no liberty. . . ." Where Locke advocated the protection of liberty by the assertion of the rights of man,

Montesquieu advocated the establishment of the principle of the separation of powers.

The Purpose of Laws

An English judge, Sir William Blackstone, published in 1765 his *Commentaries on the Laws of England* in which he set forth his view on civil government. He also analyzed and explained the common law of England, which is the basis of American law. In his observations on liberty and government, he followed Locke and Montesquieu rather closely. He said that since "the principal aim of society is to protect individuals in the enjoyment of those absolute rights which were vested in them by the immutable laws of nature . . . the first and primary end of human laws is to maintain and regulate these 'absolute' rights of individuals." Civil liberty he defined as "natural liberty so far restrained by human laws (and no further) as is necessary and expedient for the general advantage of the public." The government could achieve this objective by preserving life, liberty, and property.

In the philosophies of such learned men as Locke, Montesquieu, and Blackstone we have an important part of the background of the Constitution. Much of their teachings were given the sanction of law by the framers of our Constitution.

The Magna Carta, the Petition of

BLACKSTONE

Right, the Bill of Rights, the philosophies of Locke, Montesquieu, and Blackstone, and the consummation of centuries of bloodshed and sacrifice, formed the foundation upon which the architects built our Constitution.

TOPICAL OUTLINE FOR STUDY

A. Background of Constitution in English Documents
  1. Magna Carta, 1215
  2. Petition of Right, 1628
  3. Bill of Rights, 1689
B. Philosophical Background of Constitution
  1. John Locke, *Treatises on Government*
    (a) Natural rights of man: life, liberty, and property
    (b) Four limitations on legislatures imperative in order to achieve good government
      (i) Legislature must rule according to laws of nature.
      (ii) Legislature must not transgress the written laws.
      (iii) Legislature cannot take property from an individual except with the individual's consent.
      (iv) Legislature cannot transfer to another agency power to make laws.
  2. Montesquieu
    (a) Doctrine of the separation of the powers of government as essential to the preservation of liberty
    (b) His concept of liberty
  3. Sir William Blackstone, *Commentaries on the Laws of England*
    (a) Basis of American law
    (b) His concept of civil liberty
    (c) Aim of society

QUESTIONS

1. What kind of government had mankind failed to construct prior to 1788?
2. Why is the Magna Carta important to the people of the United States?
3. What four fundamental principles of government did the Magna Carta establish?
4. What four fundamental principles of liberty were set forth in the Petition of Right?
5. How did political liberty triumph in England through the Bill of Rights?
6. In what amendments to the Constitution of the United States do we find the influence of the Petition of Right and the Bill of Rights?
7. Who was John Locke and what was his philosophy on the natural rights of man?
8. What four limitations on legislatives bodies did John Locke regard as imperative?
9. How did John Locke influence the Constitution of the United States?
10. Who was the author of *Spirit of the Laws?*
11. What was the influence of the *Spirit of the Laws* on the Constitution of the United States?
12. What book did Blackstone write and what was its influence on American law?
13. Explain Blackstone's concept of civil liberty.
14. Name the three great documents and the three philosophers who profoundly affected the principles of the Constitution of the United States.

Early Jamestown

CHAPTER 2

The Colonial Background

Part One EARLY COLONIES

Equally important in the Constitution's background was the experience of the American colonists from the founding of the first colony in 1607 to the Declaration of Independence in 1776. God, gold, and glory were motivating forces in the exploration and colonization of the New World. America was settled by individuals who were seeking freedom from the restraints of the Old World. Some were seeking adventure, while others sought escape from poverty and religious persecution. Many perished—victims of climate, disease, starvation, and the Indians. How these pioneers in America built a free government dedicated to the promotion of the public welfare is, as we stated in the opening paragraphs, one of the most soul-stirring epics of mankind.

From 1607 to 1776, the colonies lived under charters consisting of written statements of the rights, privileges, and manner of government of each colony. Allegiance to the fundamental principles of government set forth in these charters (and later in the thirteen state constitutions, and still later in the Constitution of the United States) established firmly in the minds of Americans the value of a written constitution and of a government with limited powers.

The First Colony

Virginia was the first English colony in America. The story of the struggle of the Virginia settlers for self-government is a splendid example of the experiences of the early American with governing institutions. A corporation known as the London Company was organized for the purpose of colonizing a portion of America. The king of England granted to this company a charter guaranteeing to all members of the colony the right of trial by jury and the protection of English law. In addition, it specified the type of government that the Virginia colony should have, control being vested in the king, who appointed a governing body resident in England.

This body, consisting of thirteen members, was known as the Superior Council of Virginia. It was empowered to select thirteen men in Virginia to serve as the Resident Council for governing

13

the colony and executing five specific duties: first, to elect annually a president; second, to make rules for governing the colony until they should be cancelled by the king; third, to administer justice as a court of law; fourth, to appoint whatever public officials were deemed necessary to carry on the government; and fifth, to administer the affairs of local communities.

Arbitrary Rule

Such was the type of government in Virginia from the founding of Jamestown to 1609. However, the harshness of the wilderness, the lack of food, the hostile Indians, the internal dissension of the colony, jealousy, and disease nearly brought ruin to the settlement. The Resident Council was abolished at that time, and the Superior Council in England sent a governor, Sir Thomas Dale, to rule with military authority.

The arbitrary and tyrannical rule of this governor from 1611 to 1616 was never equaled in American colonial history. Everyone was compelled to work at an assigned task. There was no recognition of individual ownership of land or produce under this system. Food was bad, and the lazy became dependents instead of self-supporting colonists. The industrious and thrifty voiced objections to this "ownership in common," but those who resisted Governor Dale were shot as traitors, burned at the stake, or broken on a "wheel."

Realizing that this early experiment in common ownership was an utter failure, the governor abolished the common store in 1614. He inaugurated a new system that assigned land for private development. However, the government still owned the land and controlled it to a large extent. Despite the arbitrary rule of Sir Thomas Dale, order and discipline were established in the settlement, and the colonists began to acknowledge the fact that their survival depended upon hard work.

Edwin Sandys

Dissatisfaction continued even after the succession of Governor Argall in 1617. The people grew restless under a regime that excluded them from participation in government and from complete and unrestricted ownership of land. This regime of exclusion of the rights of the colonists, however, was nearing its end. In 1618 the control of the London Company experienced a "change of hands." With a change favorable to the Virginia settlement there appeared upon the scene one of the unsung heroes of American self-government, Sir Edwin Sandys, who had served as treasurer of the London Company. He was the son of the Archbishop of York, an attorney and a member of the English Parliament, where he was noted for his antagonistic attitude toward arbitrary government. Accident of circumstance brought Sandys and his followers into control of the London Company at the height of dissatisfaction in Virginia. They looked upon Virginia not only as a place for business profits but also as an opportunity for political experiment. Martial law and the program of common ownership were terminated as quickly as possible by the new regime. Sir George Yeardley, who had ruled Virginia in the interim between Dale and Argall, was sent as governor from England with a new plan of government and land ownership.

On April 19, 1619, the governor announced the complete abolition of the existing land system. Each colonist was given a tract of land. Those who had been in the colony before 1616 received a hundred acres. Those who had arrived after that date were allotted fifty acres. Firm in his belief that the colony could succeed only with self-government, Sandys instructed Governor Yeardley to call together a representative assembly for the purpose of governing the colony. The governor, six councilors appointed by the London Company, and two burgesses (citizens) from each community or plantation were to meet for the purpose of making laws.

House of Burgesses

Comprised of twenty-two elected representatives, the first House of Burgesses convened on July 30, 1619, and remained in session until August 9, 1619, when the governor adjourned the assembly until March of the following year. Prayer opened the session of the first gathering, a custom which has been continued to our day at the opening of a legislative assembly. The first business before the assembly was that of the determination of the qualifications of its members, a right that the House of Commons had won from the king. It is interesting to note that the legislative right is guaranteed today to the state legislatures by the fifty state constitutions and to the Congress by the Constitution of the United States. In addition to the laws against the recognized criminal offenses, laws were passed against "excess in apparell," idleness, gambling, swearing, and drunkenness. Production of silk, flax, and wine was encouraged in ordinances. Provision was made for the taxation of every male over sixteen years of age in the colony at one pound of tobacco or its equivalent each year.

Virginia House of Burgesses

Thus were the legislative decisions of the first representative assembly in America written into the annals of history. With the Virginia House of Burgesses leading the way as the first representative assembly, every colony was destined to achieve this self-governing institution.

The Virginia government had now taken permanent shape. Its

executive head was the governor appointed by the London Company (and later on by the king when Virginia became a royal colony). The governor was aided by six councilors appointed in theory by the Company (and later by the king) but in practice by the governor. The governor and council performed executive functions, acted as the upper house of the legislature, and sat as a court of last resort. The House of Burgesses was the lower house of the legislature. This pattern of government became the precedent for each of the other twelve American colonies.

A Threatened Setback

Granting of such self-governing institutions to Virginia was too large a concession in one swoop for King James I to tolerate. Internal politics in England led to a clash between the enlightened leaders of the Company and the king. On June 16, 1624, Virginia became a royal colony subject to the will of the king. Abolition of the House of Burgesses was the intention, but in 1625 King James died before he could act. His successor, Charles I, seeking to gain a tobacco monopoly, allowed the House to continue, and representative government became a permanent part of American life.

Tyranny and Rebellion

The reactions of Virginians to governors who denied them their rights as Englishmen is clearly illustrated by their treatment of Governor Harvey (1629-1635). His refusal to allow the House of Burgesses to petition the king for a redress of their grievances in a tobacco contract, and his threats to imprison members of his council and the House who were not in agreement with his policies, incited the people to send Harvey back to England escorted by two burgesses. The king returned him temporarily to the colony (1637-1638), but the temper of the people soon brought about his dismissal.

Probably the best-known colonial governor of Virginia was Sir William Berkeley, who held office between 1641-1653 and 1658-1677. By keeping his assembly fourteen years without any elections during his second administration, he succeeded in concentrating governmental control in the hands of a very few. This situation, together with a drop in the price of tobacco, brought a feeling of hopelessness to the colonists.

In 1675 and 1676 an Indian war broke out. Governor Berkeley made no determined attempt to protect the settlers who were demanding vigorous opposition to the Indians. The people accused him of profiting in the Indian trade. The colonists then enlisted their own soldiers under the leadership of Nathaniel Bacon, a young planter, who led his men into the Indian war. He was declared a traitor by the governor. When the people rose in wrath, Berkeley fearfully granted their demands to pardon their leader and to elect a new assembly. However, disagreements between the two men soon led to Bacon's Rebellion, which terminated in the burning of Jamestown and the death of Bacon. Berkeley succeeded in crushing the rebellion, but his ruthless beheading of many of Bacon's followers resulted in his recall by Charles II.

Bacon's Rebellion was significant because the people acted for themselves against arbitrary and corrupt government. They compelled the governor to call an election of an assembly responsive to the will of the people. They forced the dismissal of the governor and asserted their dislike of "bad" government. Successors of Berkeley were forced to redress grievances of the people before the assembly would pass measures recommended by the governor. Early in Virginia's history representative self-government was established and the people became vigilant in preserving it.

Sir William Berkeley

The Pilgrims

While the *Mayflower* was still at sea off the bleak shores of New England, on November 11, 1620, the immortal Mayflower Compact was struck from the pen of the Pilgrim Fathers. Acknowledging allegiance to the king of England, the Pilgrims pledged themselves in a "civil Body Politick" to obey "such just and equal Laws, Ordinances, Acts, Constitutions, and Offices, from time to time, as shall be thought most meet and convenient for the general Good of the Colony." This was not a constitution. It was merely an agreement to provide order until some form of political authority was prescribed by the king. Inasmuch as such authority was not forthcoming, the Plymouth Colony was destined to be governed under the Mayflower Compact until William III annexed it to Massachusetts Bay Colony in 1691. In the meantime, the colony developed a structure of government very similar to that of Virginia, its basic difference being that the colony was completely self-governing.

Before leaving Europe, the Pilgrims had formed an agreement with their financial sponsors providing that for seven years the fruits of their labor should go into a common fund, or store, from which they were to be fed and clothed. At the end of the seven years there was to be an equal division of the fund, or store, in the form of houses, lands, and cash. As long as Plymouth operated under this system, the Pilgrims were constantly faced with the danger of starvation. Indus-

Nathaniel Bacon

trious men would not stand by and see the results of their labor used to feed the families of less active and laborious men. They objected to their wives being ordered to do tasks for other men, such as washing, housekeeping, and preparing meals.

Nothing but disaster for the colonists loomed from this communal plan, so in 1623 (long before the communal experiment was to have ended) the system of private property was initiated. Governor Bradford tells us that the whole spirit of the colony changed quickly. Everybody became more industrious. The effect of this system of private property was that of a hypodermic injection in the veins of the settlement and undoubtedly saved the Pilgrims from ultimate extermination.

The Puritans

While Plymouth was establishing the concepts of private property, the Puritans founded Massachusetts Bay Colony. Under the leadership of John Endicott, in 1628, the colony of Salem was founded. A turn of events in England in the following year led to an abundant migration of Puritans to America. Charles I had dissolved Parliament, which was controlled by the Puritans, and imprisoned its leaders. Feeling their situation to be hopeless in England, the Puritans turned to America as the place where they might enjoy political liberty and worship God as they saw fit. Accordingly, they appealed to the Massachusetts Bay Company, a majority of whose stockholders were Puritans. The charter of

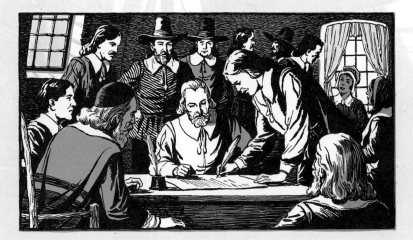

the company, by permission of the English courts, was taken to Massachusetts, and John Winthrop was elected governor. By 1630, Boston and several other towns were founded by the 2,000 new Puritan settlers. In the eleven years from 1629 to 1640 some 25,000 Puritans settled in the Massachusetts Bay Colony.

The Government of the Puritans

Under the terms of the charter, the government of the colony was vested in the officers of the company. Twelve men, with Winthrop as their leader, were empowered to govern and rule. In each of the governor's assistants were vested the powers of an English justice of the peace. At first Winthrop attempted to rule with little consideration for the freemen (men admitted to full political privileges). The result was many years of strife for religious toleration and political freedom on the part of those entitled to the status of freemen. A protest against Winthrop's and his assistants' manner of rule came from the small community of Watertown as a result of tax assessments for the construction of forts. The freemen of Watertown considered this to be "taxation without representation."

In 1632 provision was made for the annual election of the governor and his assistants. Also, no taxes were to be levied unless a general assembly was held in which each town had two elected representatives. In 1634 the Massachusetts Bay Colony adopted the representative principle of government. The General Court, consisting of the governor and assistants, henceforth was to have two representatives from each town with the power of making laws, electing the governor and assistants, and levying taxes. In unseating Winthrop and electing a new governor, the General Court used the written ballot for the first time in American history.

In 1635 the representatives demanded a written code of laws. After much delay the code was completed and was known as the "Body of Liberties." It guaranteed the right of trial by jury and provided that no person could be punished except for violation of some specific law of the colony. Right of petition for redress of grievances was given to everyone in the colony. Religious freedom and political liberty in the Massachusetts Bay Colony were not complete, however. This resulted in the establishment of other colonies, such as Rhode Island and Connecticut. Religious freedom for all Protestants was only established after the abdication of James II, when the Massachusetts Bay Colony was given a new charter as a royal colony in 1691 by King William, re-establishing free-governing institutions which had been forfeited by the colony in 1684, when all New England had been united under the governorship of Sir Edmund Andros.

Part Two   COLONIAL GOVERNMENT—OUR HERITAGE

Representation of the people in their colonial assemblies became a basic characteristic of the colonial governments. By 1776 all colonies were operating under some form of organized government. Eight (Virginia, South and North Carolina, Massachusetts Bay Colony, Georgia, New York, New Jersey, and New Hampshire) were royal colonies, being directly responsible to the king. Three (Pennsylvania, Maryland, and Delaware) were proprietary, being owned by individuals under grant of the king. Two (Connecticut and Rhode Island) were self-governing, the king allowing these colonies to elect all of their own officers and make their own laws.

Division of Powers

The political experience of the colonies formed an important part of the background of the framers of the Constitution.

Three general departments of government (executive, judicial, and legislative) were considered a necessary principle by the colonists. Written into the Constitution, that same principle remains to this day one of the fundamental characteristics of our form of government. The colonists believed implicitly that separate officials should carry out the functions of these three divisions.

In the royal and proprietary colonies, the colonial governors were important cogs in the machinery of government. They constituted the avenue of communication between the colony and the mother country, but in clashes between the two, the governor's obligation was to the king. In theory only were important legislative powers exercised by the governor. Originally, he possessed the right to initiate laws, but conflicts with the people had whittled that power down to the right merely to send messages recommending the passage of laws.

Limitation of that power is of great significance because to this very day *no American executive can directly initiate laws.* He can only send recommendations to the legislative bodies, even though he may *indirectly* influence legislation through various aspects of his executive powers and his political position as head of his party.

Powers of the Governor

Executive Control of Legislatures

The governor had power to convene, adjourn, or dissolve the legislative body of the colony. Strong governors used this power as a "big stick" to keep the colonial assemblies in line with their own selfish interests. Assemblies could be maintained in office as long as the governors pleased or could be dissolved when they desired. Attempting to eliminate that condition, the colonists tried unsuccessfully to have England establish a definite date for the election of assemblies.

This bitter experience impressed our Constitutional fathers with the necessity for providing *a stated time for the meeting of*

Congress. Similar precaution in regard to the election of state legislatures was taken in the state constitutions.

The Absolute Veto

The vesting of absolute power of veto in the royal governor was also a source of great annoyance to the colonists, and threw the governor and assembly into a veritable tug of war. Added to this was the fact that many times, laws agreed to by the governor were later vetoed by the king. In the Declaration of Independence, the complaint was made against the king that "He has refused his Assent to Laws, the most wholesome and necessary for the public good."

Later on in our history considerable debate occurred in the Constitutional Convention over whether the President should be given absolute or limited veto power. Mindful of colonial experience, the framers gave the President limited veto power and empowered Congress to override him by a two-thirds vote of both Houses.

District Representation

Another of the governor's powers was his right to determine the boundaries of districts from which representatives were elected. By proper arrangement of districts, representatives friendly to the governor could be elected. But this loophole of undue influence of the executive over the legislature was checked in the Constitution by the provision that the legislature of each state should determine the manner of election of members of Congress.

The colonial governor many times appointed a representative to a colonial administrative job, making the appointee an administrative officer as well as a legislator. This effectively blocked any practice of separation of powers. Dual officeholding of this nature, however, was abolished by the Constitution and also by the constitutions of the several states.

Without the elimination of these unsound practices the preservation of liberty would have been only a dream instead of a reality. The ultimate restrictions upon the powers of colonial governors played an important role in the dramatic creation of a representative, republican government in America.

Other Powers

The powers of pardon, land grants, the establishment of markets, fairs, and ports were all powers exercised by the governor. He was commander in chief of the military forces of the colony. One power of the colonial governor that has been handed down to the executive of today was his right to appoint officials to administrative posts. Used in that day to build a political following, this power of the executive retains its use to the present day. Because he appointed judicial officers and because of his position as the presiding justice of the colonial court of last resort, he possessed judicial authority. In each colony there was a governor's council of approximately 12 members for the purpose of aiding the governor in the administration of the affairs of the colony. The constitutional provision requiring the advice and consent of the Senate to presidential appointments is a development from the colonial requirement that the governor's appointments be confirmed by the council.

Rise of the Legislatures

It has already been noted that each colony possessed a representative assembly. Two rights were attained by that branch of the government: First, it initiated the laws; and second, no money could be raised without its consent. Control of the "purse strings" was kept in the hands of the people through the assemblies. In England as early as 1628, when Charles I was forced to approve the Petition of Right as a result of Parliament's refusal to appropriate funds for his kingdom, Englishmen had been impressed with the fact that "money talks" with remarkable conviction. The American colonists did not hesitate to make use of this effective power when they wished to compel governors to follow their will. Colonial governors were dependent on their assemblies for the appropriations necessary to carry on the government, including their salaries.

Fearless and daring use of the "purse string" power by these assemblies enabled them seriously to restrain the governor's power and increase the spirit of independence. By the outbreak of the Revolution in 1776 the colonial assemblies had come to possess a dominating place in the structure of colonial government.

Seeking immunity from any executive domination which could seriously interfere with the liberties of the colony, the colonial assemblies assumed some powers which were identical to those which the House of Commons had acquired in England. The two

New England Town Meeting

outstanding illustrations of this were their rights to initiate legislation and to originate tax levies.

The history of these assemblies is the history of a long chain of disputes between governor and assembly. Some of these disputes revolved about the designation of the colonial treasurer, the appointment of the speaker, the control of appropriations and the salaries of colonial officials, and the authorization of payments of money without the governor's warrant. Colonial political leadership apparently was forging its own way into the administration of colonial affairs and demanding the fulfillment of its own desires.

A decided feeling of distrust of the executive grew up. The people of the colonies trusted their legislatures and looked upon them as their protectors against arbitrary government. This tendency was apparent in the first state constitutions after the Revolution.

Local Government

Local government existed in three forms. In New England, the center of government was the town. As early as 1633 the towns of Massachusetts Bay Colony set aside one day each month when the freeman assembled to discuss the town affairs. They elected their own officers, voted taxes, chose their representatives to the colonial assembly, and debated governmental policies. Town affairs were managed by a Board of Selectmen and its moderator, town clerk, constables, assessors, treasurer, school trustees, and surveyors. The colonial government held the town responsible for the maintenance of the militia, schools, roads, bridges, and police regulations. Anyone could attend the town meeting and speak his mind, but only the freemen had the right to vote. "Freemen" were all males of age who had taken an oath of allegiance to the colony and its laws and been admitted into membership of the Company of Massachusetts Bay.

In Virginia and other areas of the South the population was not concentrated in towns. Plantations were the method of agricultural development, and population was necessarily more or less scattered. The unit of local government was the county. The sheriff, justices of the peace, and the commander of the militia were the important county officers and were appointed by the governor. Administration of county governmental functions was charged to the county court. In the middle colonies, a form of government which was a combination of these two was developed.

The day-to-day activities of government—such as maintenance of schools, care of the poor, assessment and collection of taxes, and the construction and operation of roads and bridges—the colonists felt could best be administered by themselves through local governing agencies. They came to regard local self-government as essential to the preservation of their liberty. The smaller the unit of government, the more easily they could check and control the power of their officers.

The Result of Experience

The advent of the American Revolution found the thirteen colonies with similar political experience. Their governing institutions had been the results of this experience from 1607 to 1776. One hundred and seventy years had given them ample opportunity to test the efficiency of these institutions. During that time, they had learned to value local self-government as the backbone of the entire governmental structure. Through their charters they learned the worth of written constitutions, because the limited powers of government as set forth in written constitutions proved to be the practical device for the preservation of their hard-won political liberty.

TOPICAL OUTLINE FOR STUDY

A. Evolution of Self-Government in the Colony of Virginia
   1. Government by the London Company, 1607-1609
   2. Government by a governor with military authority, 1609-1618
   3. House of Burgesses, 1619
     (a) Sir Edwin Sandys
     (b) Governor Yeardley
   4. Virginia, a royal colony, 1624
   5. Virginia's reaction to arbitrary governors
     (a) Governor Harvey
     (b) Sir William Berkeley and Bacon's Rebellion
     (c) Representative self-government established
B. Evolution of Self-Government in the Massachusetts Bay Colony
   1. Mayflower Compact, 1620
   2. Plymouth Colony
   3. Puritans in Massachusetts Bay Colony
   4. Massachusetts Bay Colony under Governor Winthrop

5. Massachusetts Bay Colony General Court, 1634
6. Massachusetts Bay Colony Body of Liberties
7. Arbitrary rule of Governor Andros
8. Representative self-government
C. Charters Under Which the Colonies Operated in 1776
   1. Royal
   2. Proprietary
   3. Self-governing
D. Influence of Colonial Experience on the Constitution
   1. Limitation of the power of the executive
   2. Powers vested in the legislative branch of the government
     (a) Initiated all the laws
     (b) No money could be raised without the legislature's consent
   3. Local self-government
     (a) Town
     (b) County
     (c) Combination of both

QUESTIONS

1. What was the nature of the individuals who settled America?
2. What was the London Company and how did it govern the colony of Virginia from 1607 to 1618?
3. What was the significance of the establishment of the House of Burgesses in Virginia in 1619?
4. Describe the reaction of Virginians to arbitrary governors.
5. How did Bacon's Rebellion affect the struggle for self-government in Virginia?
6. What were the provisions of the Mayflower Compact?
7. How did the communal experiment work out in Plymouth Colony?
8. Describe the struggle for self-government in Massachusetts Bay Colony under Governor Winthrop.
9. What were the three types of colonies existing in 1776, and what were the characteristics of each?
10. Compare the powers of the colonial governor with the powers of the President of the United States.

11. What were the two fundamental rights possessed by the legislatures of the colonies? Why are they important?
12. Why did the colonists distrust the executive?
13. Describe the three forms of local self-government which existed in the America of 1776.
14. Why did the political experience of the colonists form an important part of the background of the framers of the Constitution?

Samuel Adams   Sons of Liberty   Paul Revere

CHAPTER 3

The Development of the Idea of Union

The dual nature of our government, the state on the one hand and the nation on the other, had its origin in colonial days. Since each colony started as a separate settlement, the social system and economic interests of each were provincial. Lack of easy methods of transportation and communication emphasized these differences and stimulated fear and envy of one another. Commercial competition and religious differences set up barriers of isolation which were difficult to overcome. Most important of all, from the standpoint of politics, was the fact that each colony lived under its own charter and developed its own governmental system. Each

31

colony regarded itself as a separate country, and men were proud of their allegiance to their colony.

Common Dangers

Tending to break down this feeling of separation were the common dangers from the Indians, the French, and the Dutch. The struggle between England and France for supremacy over the North American Continent did much to bring the colonists together and break down the provincial attitude that prevailed. Their mutual allegiance to England gave them a common political experience and led to the development of a similar legal system. By the time of the Revolution a common political philosophy had been developed. The fact that a permanent union under the Constitution was finally effected was not due to accident. It was the result of the evolution of the idea of unity. This was finally established under a system that reserved all governing powers to the states except those necessary to facilitate the operation of the national government.

New England Confederation

As a result of the menace of the Indians and the Dutch, we find the first attempt at union by the New England settlements in 1643. Massachusetts Bay Colony, Plymouth, New Haven, and Connecticut formed the *New England Confederation* for the protection of their mutual interests. Their main purpose was both a defensive and offensive military alliance against the Indians and the Dutch. Into the constitution of this Confederation was written a provision that the members would carry on the propagation of the truths and liberties of the gospel and would work for mutual safety and welfare, seeking to attain protection for all. Invitations to join the confederation were extended to the other colonies.

Powers of First Union

A governing body consisting of eight commissioners was created and vested with authority, first, to declare a state of war; second, to provide for the division of the spoils of war; third, to determine the basis for the admission of other colonies; fourth, to see to the extradition of criminals or fugitives from one colony to the other;

fifth, to settle disputes among the members of the confederation; and sixth, an elastic clause, reading: "All things of like nature which are proper consequence of such Confederation for amity, offense and defense."

In a crude way this cause suggests the "elastic" clause of the federal Constitution which confers upon Congress the power "to make all Laws which shall be necessary and proper for carrying into Execution the foregoing Powers. . . ." Also, the Confederation's power to extradite criminals and fugitives may be regarded as the pattern for the constitutional sections providing for the return of criminals and fugitive servants to the state having jurisdiction over them.

For about ten years, the confederation functioned with some degree of success. Apportionment of troops and money for defense and support of the confederation was on the basis of population. As the Massachusetts Bay Colony grew in population, her quota of fighting men and her increase in costs led her on numerous occasions to refuse to participate in several of the Indian wars. Eventually the confederation collapsed.

New England Dominion

The next attempt at union came as part of England's plan to gain better governing control over the colonies and to unify them for war with France and the Indians. In 1688, she tried to consolidate the New England colonies with New York and New Jersey under the *New England Dominion*. The king proceeded to cancel the charters of each colony in the dominion. The character of the government was arbitrary, with no provision for a representative assembly. The governor, Sir Edmund Andros, was appointed by the king. To the governor was given full power to levy taxes, regulate the public lands, make laws, administer justice, and to be commander in chief of the military and naval forces. In the organization of this Dominion, the first major difficulty between England and her colonies began. People who objected to taxation without being represented in a representative assembly were jailed without legal process. With the ascension of William and Mary to the throne, the charters were restored, the Dominion coming to an end.

Penn Plan

Colonial union could not be forced by England under a plan which destroyed colonial liberty and self-government, so William Penn in 1696 conceived the *Penn Plan* with the objectives of colonial harmony, safeguarding commerce, and promoting general tranquility. He proposed that the king appoint a high commissioner and that two delegates be elected from each colony to a colonial assembly. Power to legislate upon matters which affected all colonies—such as defense against their foes, extradition, and commercial regulations—was vested in the assembly. Fearing that representative, self-governing institutions might be destroyed under the plan, the colonists were unwilling to follow Penn.

Albany Plan of Union

In 1754 a conference of all the New England colonies, as well as New York, Pennsylvania, and Maryland, was held for the purpose of renewing the treaties with the Iroquois Indians. Benjamin Franklin, the greatest American of that day, presented his *Albany Plan of Union*. It called for the formation of a colonial union to be governed by a president-general appointed by the king and an assembly known as the Grand Council elected from each colony on a basis of wealth. The Grand Council was to have control over Indian affairs, levy taxes, and protect and defend the colonists. Adopted by the conference, the Plan was submitted to England and each colonial assembly for approval. England rejected it on the ground that it would give the colonies too much self-government. Each colonial assembly rejected it because of the possibility that the privileges and liberties of the

William Penn

Benjamin Franklin

people could be wiped out under such a union.

Thus, four plans (New England Confederation of 1643, the New England Dominion of 1688, the Penn Plan of 1696, and the Albany Plan of 1754) to unify the American colonies had failed. But after 1754, England's attempt to regulate colonial commerce through the navigation acts and her efforts to levy taxes on the Americans drove the colonies more and more to united action against the mother country's oppression. The fear of losing some of their rights had kept the colonies separate, but an even greater desire to preserve their right of self-government was to bring them together.

The Stamp Act

Parliament, in 1765, attempted to collect taxes in the colonies by passing the Stamp Act, which levied a tax on all documents used in the colonies. The response of the colonists was refusal to purchase the stamps that were to be affixed to the documents. Immediately the cry became: "No taxation without representation." It was at this time that Patrick Henry

Patrick Henry

came forth with a barrage of eloquence denouncing tyrannical government and driving the Virginia House of Burgesses to the adoption of a set of resolutions against the stamp tax.

Henry's challenge to the mother country roused men by its ringing tone of warning. In response to Virginia's action, Massachusetts issued a call for a congress of delegates from each of the colonies to meet in the City of New York. On October 7, 1765, delegates from nine colonies convened and drew up a petition to Parliament protesting the stamp tax and demanding its repeal. As Englishmen, they denied the existence of any right of Parliament to tax them because they were not represented in Parliament. Since they were represented only in their colonial assemblies, they boldly held that the exclusive right of taxing them reposed in the assemblies alone. The significance of the Stamp Act Congress lies in the fact that it was an expression of the existence of an American nationality. "Join or die" became the slogan of many who were seeking to preserve "the natural rights of man."

Military Control Re-established

Violent reaction to the tax was aroused in the colonies. Stamp collectors were forced to resign. Their offices were ransacked and burned. Under the leadership of organizations such as the "Sons of Liberty," secret committees were organized in each colony to pledge mutual allegiance and to keep one another informed.

Samuel Adams

England repealed the Stamp Act, but Parliament declared it had the right to tax the colonies and regulate their commerce. Attempts to tax America by England continued. But always the colonists resisted, standing on British constitutional ground that there could be "no taxation without representation." England stubbornly stood its ground and sent garrisons to America, notably to Boston, where the presence of the headquarters of British customs commissioners was causing trouble,

Boston Tea Party

for Samuel Adams was making Massachusetts a center of opposition. English action stirred the ire of the people and eventually led to an unfortunate event, the Boston Massacre. Passage of the Townshend Acts—taxing tea, glass, lead, and paper—brought colonial protests. These acts were repealed, and Lord North's tea tax was passed. The attempt to collect this tea tax, culminating in the Boston Tea Party, inspired England with a grim determination to "restore order" in America and to establish military rule, thus wiping out the self-governing institutions which had been the pride and joy of every freeman in America.

Two Fundamental Concepts

In the long controversy over their governing rights the colonists had based their contentions on two fundamental concepts. First, they believed in the *"natural rights of man"* and that the only way in which these rights could be preserved was by a *free government with well-defined restricted powers.* John Adams' statement of the rights of the colonists had become the popular philoso-

37

phy of the hour: "You have rights antecedent to all earthly governments; rights that cannot be repealed or restrained by human laws; rights derived from the Great Legislator of the Universe." Second, although they did not deny that their allegiance was to the king and Parliament, they maintained that Parliament was sovereign only within a particular field of government and that the colonial assemblies were sovereign in their sphere. Thus had been born the *concept of dual government,* the very foundation stone of the relationship of our present federal and state governments.

Intolerable Acts

England's avowed policy of punishment of Massachusetts for the Boston Tea Party manifested itself in the passage of the Intolerable Acts by Parliament. The port of Boston was blockaded. Massachusetts' local and self-governing institutions were abolished. Persons accused of major criminal offenses were transferred to England for trial. Troops were quartered in the private homes of citizens. The Great Northwest Territory was taken away from the colonists through the Quebec Act and made a part of Canada.

First Continental Congress

Common action by all the colonies was now imperative. Through the committees on correspondence, a united front was attempted. The response was immediate. Pledging aid to Massachusetts, all except Georgia answered the Virginia call for the First Continental Congress at Philadelphia to convene September 5, 1774. To this great Congress came the great leaders of the American Revolution: George Washington, Patrick Henry, Peyton Randolph, and Richard Lee of Virginia, John Jay from New York, and 51 other delegates. Without losing a precious moment the Congress got down to business immediately. It issued a Declaration of Resolves and Grievances protesting the action of England with regard to Massachusetts and asserted the rights of the colonists to preserve their natural rights under the British Constitution and under their

Old North Church

charters. The Congress made it very clear to the mother country that if the grievances of the colonies were not redressed, it would convene again in May of 1775.

Most effective in the accomplishments of the Congress was an agreement among the colonies to restrict all trade with England. It was agreed in signing the Continental Association that after December 1, 1774, import of British goods would be prohibited and that nonexportation of colonial goods to Great Britain or its possessions would become effective in September of the following year.

Independence Hall

Second Continental Congress

Having thus forged the first link of the chain in their united front against the British, the colonists enforced the provisions of the Association in an effective manner through local committees. The choice of revolution or conciliation was put up to the discretion of the mother country by the colonists. Despite the efforts of Pitt and Burke, no attention was given to the demand for redress of grievances. Britain was determined to teach the "infant protesters" in America a lesson with the sword. But much to the embarrassment of the Redcoats, they found them to be students of a very uncooperative nature. By the time the Second Continental Congress convened at Philadelphia on May 10, 1775, the Revolution had broken out in Massachusetts. British troops left Boston one night to destroy colonial military supplies. Warned by the signal from Old North Church, Paul Revere and William Dawes warned the minutemen, who battled the British troops at Lexington and Concord. Even though Lexington and Concord

39

had been fought, members of the Congress still hoped that reconciliation would take place. The Continental Congress, composed of such popular heroes as Samuel Adams, John Hancock, and Thomas Jefferson, did not immediately undertake a declaration of independence. The seriousness of the situation facing the colonists, however, was not overlooked. Forces of the Continental Army were placed under the direction of George Washington as commander in chief. Another petition was sent to England, and Congress adjourned in August to await further developments.

England's course of action gave the colonists little hope for consideration of their demands. Proclamations issued by the king prohibiting all trade with the colonies and declaring the Americans to be rebels ended American attempts at conciliation. When the Continental Congress convened again on September 13, 1775, many colonial leaders who had been hopeful of appeasement and had cautioned against independence were now thoroughly convinced that separation from England was the only course remaining to America.

Separate colonies gradually overthrew their colonial governors and organized committees to rule in their place. *Congress* became the *central government* of the colonies for carrying on the Revolution, and committees to handle foreign affairs and to make proper approach to foreign powers were appointed. A navy was created and bills of credit were issued. The management of Indian affairs was undertaken and also the operation of the colonial postal system. Colonies were instructed to set up their own governments by the adoption of state constitutions. Finally, on July 4, 1776, Congress, speaking for the thirteen states, agreed to the Declaration of Independence.

Reasons for Revolution

Here was a clear statement of the reasons for the Revolution. Separation from England was justified therein and the privilege of mankind to preserve its natural rights was proclaimed. This pronouncement by the Americans on human rights reads as follows:

Thomas Jefferson

(1) "That all men are created equal,

(2) that they are endowed by their Creator with certain unalienable Rights,

(3) that among these are Life, Liberty and the pursuit of Happiness.

(4) That to secure these rights, Governments are instituted among Men, deriving their just powers from the consent of the governed;

(5) That whenever any Form of Government becomes destructive of these ends it is the Right of the People to alter or to abolish it, and to institute new Government, laying its foundation on such principles, and organizing its powers in such form, as to them shall seem most likely to effect their Safety and Happiness."

The Declaration of Independence united the colonies, and the war became a war for the establishment of a nation.

TOPICAL OUTLINE FOR STUDY

A. Factors Tending to Unify the Colonies
   1. Common dangers
      (a) Indians
      (b) French
   2. Common political experience
   3. Similar legal system
B. Attempts at Union Prior to 1776

   1. New England Confederation, 1643
       (a) Structure and form of government
       (b) Practical results
       (c) Reasons for dissolution
   2. New England Dominion, 1688
       (a) Character of the government
       (b) Purpose
       (c) Reasons for failure
   3. Penn Plan of 1696
   4. Albany Plan of 1754
   5. Stamp Act of 1765
   6. First Continental Congress, 1774
       (a) Reasons for Congress
       (b) Achievement of the Congress
C. Second Continental Congress and Independence
   1. Basic causes of the Revolution
   2. Declaration of Independence

QUESTIONS

  1. Give (a) the factors which promoted disunity among the English colonies in America and (b) the factors which promoted unity.
  2. Why was the New England Confederation brought into being?
  3. What was the structure and function of the government of the New England Confederation?
  4. What influence did the New England Confederation have on certain clauses of the Constitution?
  5. Why did the New England Confederation fail?
  6. Describe the reasons for the formulation and the failure of the New England Dominion of 1688.
  7. What were the essential features of the Penn Plan of 1696?
  8. What was the Albany Plan of 1754, and why was it rejected by both the colonies and England?
  9. What was the colonists' response to the stamp tax, and how did they make their attitude effective?
 10. Upon what two fundamental concepts did the colonists base their contention for self-government?

11. Describe the events leading up to the meeting of the First Continental Congress.
12. Who were the leaders in the First Continental Congress?
13. What did the First Continental Congress achieve?
14. Set forth the numerous steps taken by the Second Continental Congress to establish American independence.
15. What did the American pronouncement on human rights declare?

VIRGINIA

CHAPTER 4

Drafting of the First State Constitutions

The drafting of the first state constitutions is a development which played an important part in the background of the federal Constitution.

During the period between the Declaration of Independence and 1780, all the states experienced the process of reorganization in their governments and the adoption of permanent state constitutions. The experience of Virginia with the framing of a state constitution is typical of that of the other states. In 1774 representatives elected by the various counties had convened to approve the work of the First Continental Congress and to put into effect the Continental Association. A second convention, in the following year, requested each county to elect delegates to a third convention which convened in Richmond and became the ruling body of Virginia. In 1776 delegates to a fourth convention were

44

elected to appoint a committee to draft a constitution for the independent state of Virginia. This constitution was destined to be one of the great state papers of American history. It gave the world the first American bill of rights.

Virginia Bill of Rights

The draftsman of the bill was George Mason, whose family had settled there in the early days of the Virginia colony. Virginia's Bill of Rights became the model for the bill of rights of other states. Section one provided: "That all men are by nature equally free and independent, and have certain inherent rights, of which, when they enter into a state of society, they cannot by any compact derive or divest their posterity; namely, the enjoyment of life and liberty, with the means of acquiring and possessing property, and pursuing and obtaining happiness and safety." Fifteen other sections proceeded to assert that all governing power is vested in the people, that three departments of government (executive, judicial, and legislative) are necessary, that all elections must be free elections, and that the inalienable rights of man (freedom of speech, of religion, of press, of trial by jury, etc.) must be respected by the government.

Virginia's New Government

Virginia's constitution set up a legislature of two houses. The lower branch (House of Delegates) was elected from counties, boroughs, and cities for a one-year term. The upper branch (Senate) was elected from districts for four-year terms, one fourth going out of office each year. All bills were to originate in the House of Delegates, but could be rejected or amended by the Senate, except in the case of money bills, which were to be accepted or rejected without amendment by the Senate. Together the two houses chose by ballot eight citizens of the state as a Privy Council to appoint delegates to the Continental Congress. Also,

Gunston Hall, George Mason's Family Home

these houses chose state judges, the secretary of state, the state treasurer, and the state attorney general.

An executive known as the governor was created and appointed by a joint vote of the legislature, subject to the approval of the Privy Council. Appointed to serve for the term of one year, the governor was eligible to hold office three years out of every seven. He possessed no power of appointment and did not have the right of veto. The judicial system was created with four types of courts: lower, chancery, general, and court of appeal to hear appeals and to pass on the constitutionality of state laws. So with the creation

Virginia State Capitol

of the three departments of government, under the constitution adopted by the convention which declared itself as the House of Delegates, Virginia was transformed from a colonial state into a sovereign state.

In response to the resolution of May 10, 1776, issued by the Continental Congress, other states set up similar systems of government differing in details but alike in principle. The congressional resolutions called on "the respective assemblies, and conventions, of the united colonies, where no government sufficient to the exigencies of their affairs has been heretofore established, to adopt such government, as should, in the opinion of the representatives of the people, best conduce to the happiness and safety of their constituents in particular and America in general."

Various State Systems

All state constitutions were adopted through legislatures except in Massachusetts and New Hampshire, where the modern method of state constitution making was employed. In these two states delegates were elected by the people to a constitutional convention for the purpose of drafting a constitution. In turn, it was voted upon by the people. Colonial charters under which they had operated were used by each state as the basis from which to construct these state documents. Connecticut and Rhode Island merely adopted their colonial charters as state constitutions.

In no states except in New England and New York were the governors actually elected by the people. They were elected by the legislature in the other states. The governor served for a term of one year, except in New York, Pennsylvania, and Delaware, where the term of office was three years, and in South Carolina, where it was two years. Practically all the powers that the governor had held as an executive officer under the colonial system of government had been taken away from him. He even lost the power to veto laws passed by the state legislature, except in the three states of Massachusetts, New York, and South Carolina. But even in these cases his veto power was limited. Colonial experience had fostered distrust in the minds of the colonists towards a gov-

Palace of the Virginia Governor

ernor who was responsible to a king thousands of miles from their shores. Americans seriously sought to restrict the powers of the governor in their state constitutions. On the other hand, the legislatures had been the representatives of the people in their fight against English oppression. Therefore, the largest amount of governmental power was placed in legislative hands. All the state constitutions exalted the legislative branch above the other two departments of state government. Connecticut and Rhode Island went so far as to vest the judicial powers in the legislature.

State Legislatures

All state legislatures consisted of two houses, with the exception of Pennsylvania and Georgia. Members of the lower branch were elected annually in all states except South Carolina, where the term was two years. In New Hampshire and Rhode Island the election was semiannual. The upper house was elected annually except in New York and Virginia, where the term was four years; Delaware, three years; Maryland, five years; and South Carolina, two years. Powers of the legislatures included the right to pass any law without the threat of a governor's veto in all states except Massachusetts, New York, and South Carolina. Extensive appointing powers were enjoyed by the upper house, while in the lower house originated all money bills. Least important of the three branches of state government was the judicial. Everywhere the judges held office by appointment of the legislature or the upper house. Term of office was "good behavior" (for as long as the judge honestly performed his duties) except in New Hampshire where it was five years; Connecticut and Rhode Island, one year; and in New Jersey and Pennsylvania, seven years.

State Constitutions

In summarizing the first state constitutions of America we find six outstanding characteristics. First, all recognized the people as

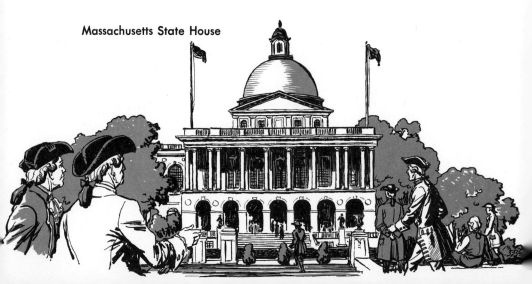

Massachusetts State House

possessing the power of political authority. Second, rotation in office was recognized as necessary to good government. Third, all recognized the doctrine of the separation of powers. Fourth, all guaranteed the rights and liberties of the individual. Fifth, there was a limitation on the right to vote based upon property and other qualifications. And sixth, the representative republican principle of government was recognized by all.

Few of these early constitutions made any provision for amendments. In some states the legislatures were empowered to make amendments and in others, such as Georgia and Massachusetts, provision was made for the calling of state constitutional conventions. The absence of an amending process in so many of these early documents has been explained by authorities as due to the fact that the framers of the state constitutions neglected the possible need for such procedure.

Maryland State Capitol

Influence of State Constitutions

The influence of the state constitutions on the federal Constitution is apparent when we realize that separation of the powers of government is basic in the national as well as state instruments of government. Experiences of the states clearly indicated that the legislature had too much power and the executive not enough for the proper functioning of government. Therefore, we find that the Constitutional Convention of 1787 conferred greater power on the President than that exercised by any governor in 1787. In order to check Congress, the President was given the power of limited veto. Elections of governors by legislatures had been unsatisfactory, hence the electoral system was devised for electing the President. The Senate was given the power to confirm the presidential appointments and the duty to ratify all treaties. The framers had learned from the operation of state constitutions that the executive must have sufficient powers to execute the laws.

Other influences are to be seen in the adoption, by the Constitutional Convention, of a representative republican government, of measures for the protection of the rights and liberties of the individual, and in the modification of the theory of rotation in office to give the Senate permanency and the President stability.

Hamilton, Madison, and Jay used the existing state constitutions as the basis of their arguments for ratification of the Constitution in *The Federalist Papers.* They did this by referring to sections of the constitutions of the several states to implement their arguments. The Convention of 1787 placed into the Constitution everything that was applicable from the state constitutions that had withstood the test of time between 1776 and 1787 and which was properly within the scope of the federal sphere or structure of government.

TOPICAL OUTLINE FOR STUDY

A. First Virginia State Constitution
  1. Bill of Rights
  2. Structure of the Virginia state government
B. Six Characteristics of the First State Constitutions in America
  1. The people—sole source of all political authority
  2. Rotation in office
  3. Separation of powers
  4. Personal rights guaranteed
  5. Limitations of the right to vote by property qualifications
  6. Representative principle of government
C. Influence of the State Constitutions on the Constitution of the United States
  1. Separation of powers
  2. Executive powers versus legislative powers
  3. Electoral system
  4. Powers of the Senate
D. Influence of the State Constitutions in the Arguments Contained in *The Federalist Papers*

QUESTIONS

1. Trace the experiences of Virginia in adopting her state constitution that were typical of the experiences of the thirteen states.
2. Into which state constitution was a bill of rights first written? Who was its author?
3. Describe fully the government of Virginia under the first Virginia constitution.
4. What recommendation did the Continental Congress make to the several states in its resolution of May 10, 1776?
5. In which of the original states was the governor elected by the direct vote of the people?
6. Why were the governors under the first state constitutions sheared of their powers?
7. What were the six outstanding characteristics of the first state constitutions?
8. What was the significance of the general absence of the "amending process" in these state constitutions?
9. Indicate along what lines the first state constitutions affected the Constitution of the United States.
10. What was the basis of the arguments in favor of the ratification of the Constitution contained in *The Federalist Papers?*

CHAPTER 5

The Articles of Confederation

The transformation of the thirteen separate states into an effective national union was no easy task.

Necessity for unity to carry on a successful war was obvious to all. The Second Continental Congress, which carried on the war, was wholly dependent upon the promulgation and enforcement of their orders by the several state legislatures. It had a difficult task. Committees were created to carry on the routine work of executive, legislative, and judicial functions. The extent of the work of the Congress in carrying out its duties is attested by the

fact that members served on as many as ninety committees. John Adams informs us that, in common with other members, he followed a rigorous schedule from four in the morning until ten in the evening. The president of the Congress carried on an enormous correspondence with the commander of the army, the governors of the states, and the agents of the Congress in the various states.

Decline of Continental Congress

Of the seven years of the war, five were carried on by this Congress, which was the only central government that existed. As the Revolution progressed, the states became more and more jealous of their own sovereignty and reluctantly acquiesced in the various demands made upon them by the Congress. Good men found it to their advantage to leave Congress and follow state politics. Many entered the diplomatic service or the army. Consequently, the caliber of the congressional membership gradually decreased. After 1778 it was difficult to achieve a quorum. States paid no attention to the demands of Congress that they fill their quota of delegates. Much of the work had to be delegated to boards and committees created outside of its own membership.

Despite these disadvantages, the Congress worked diligently to create a central government. Richard Henry Lee of Virginia, when he had introduced the resolution for the Declaration of Independence, had also introduced a resolution for the formation of a central government. From this resolution was finally drafted the Articles of Confederation.

Disagreements on Confederation

The jealousy existing among the states was clearly shown in the debate over the form of the Articles. There was disagreement in

John Adams

regard to three essential points: representation in Congress, revenues and taxation, and western lands. Provisions stating that no state should have less than two nor more than seven delegates, and that each state should have one vote, caused considerable argument. Large states insisted on representation in Congress on the basis of population or according to importance in the union. Small states objected and demanded equal representation. Questions of taxation met similar disagreement. Small states like Delaware feared absorption by the larger states if they joined a union. The large states with wealth refused to allow anybody to tax them to support the smaller states.

Resolution

Primarily, the delaying factor in the ratification of the Articles of Confederation was the controversy over western lands. Maryland insisted that all states should surrender their claims to western lands to the national government but this was not agreed upon until 1781. The Articles had been submitted for ratification on November 17, 1777, and all the states except Delaware and Maryland had approved them by 1778. Delaware agreed in 1779, and Maryland on March 1, 1781. On the following day the first Congress under the Confederation took office.

The states had been careful to specify in Article II of the Articles that: "Each state retains its sovereignty, freedom and independence, and every power, jurisdiction, and right, which is not by this Confederation expressly delegated to the United States, in Congress assembled." Thus, although a "firm league of friendship with each other" had been entered into for the maintenance of liberty and the promotion of the general welfare, there was inadequate power in the national legislature to achieve this desirable aim.

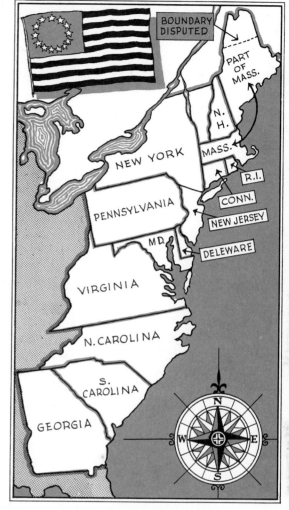

Congressional Powers

Entire executive, judicial, and legislative power was vested in the Congress of the United States. Delegates were to be elected by the state legislatures annually. Each state was to select not less than two nor more than seven delegates. Each state was to have only one vote. No person could be a delegate more than three years out of six, and members of Congress were to be compensated by the states.

Congress had the following powers: first, to control diplomatic affairs; second, to declare and wage war; third, to negotiate treaties; fourth, to requisition money from the states; fifth, to coin money and establish a system of weights and measures; sixth, to control Indian affairs; seventh, to establish a post office; eighth, to control the army and navy; ninth, to grant letters of marque and reprisal; and tenth, to establish courts to try piracies and felonies committed at sea. With slight changes these powers would be vested in Congress under the Constitution.

Three other of its provisions were destined later to be included in the federal Constitution. These were, one, free inhabitants of each state were entitled to "all privileges and immunities of free citizens in the several states"; two, extradition of fugitives from state to state was recognized; and three, provision was further made that "Full faith and credit shall be given in each of these states to the records, acts, and judicial proceedings of the courts and magistrates of every other state."

Fundamental Defects

There were numerous weaknesses in the Articles of Confederation. A fundamental defect was to be found in the absence of any power in Congress to raise revenues to meet obligations. Congress had been denied the powers to regulate national and international commerce, to levy taxes, to use force to carry out the determination of policy, and authority to prevent a state from impairing the obligations of its contracts. Every important measure or question which it was to adopt required the consent of nine states. A unanimous vote was necessary to adopt an amendment.

The Confederation was really built not upon the people of the United States but upon the states of the United States. The union, therefore, lacked a national cohesion and a centralization of power.

Aftereffects of Revolution

Having successfully negotiated the Treaty of Peace in 1783, thus terminating the Revolution, Congress was next faced with

Robert Morris

the problems of peace. The economic, social, and political reconstruction that followed the war was far from being a peaceful one. During the Revolution, the demand of both the American and English armies for foods and supplies had greatly raised the price level in the country, particularly for agricultural products. By the end of the war there was a drastic deflation of prices. New England suffered severely from a depression in its shipbuilding industry. British goods were selling at a lower price in American markets than were American-produced goods. Disbanding of the army in 1783 added to the problem of unemployment. There was discontent in many parts of the country.

Lack of Finances

We have already noted that Congress lacked the power to levy and collect taxes. From Robert Morris, who at that time was superintendent of finance, comes a sad picture of "the wolf sitting on the doorstep" of the nation: "Imagine the situation of a man who is to direct the finances of a country almost without revenue (for such you will perceive this to be) surrounded by creditors whose distresses, while they increase their clamors, render it more difficult to appease them; an army ready to disband or mutiny; a government whose sole authority consists in the power of framing recommendations."

The war had been financed by loans from France and Holland as well as from private individuals in America. Debts contracted by the United States government to carry on the war amounted to about $42,000,000. Debts contracted by the states reached around $26,000,000. In addition, approximately $250,000,000 in

57

(fiat) paper currency had also been issued by the Continental Congress. Continental currency had been made legal tender by the state legislatures. But by 1776 depreciation had set in before $20,000,000 had been issued. The purchasing power in 1776 was 12 cents on the dollar. By 1781 it was "not worth a Continental." It no longer circulated and was purchased by speculators at the rate of one dollar for one thousand.

Attempts to Raise Money

Early in 1781 Congress submitted to the states a proposal to levy a five percent import duty for the purpose of paying the principle and interest on the public debt. Rhode Island refused to ratify on the ground, first, that it would place the largest burden on the commercial states; second, that officers unaccountable to the state governments would come into the states to collect the revenue; and third, that this tax would make Congress independent of its constituents. Therefore, the proposal was "repugnant to the liberty of the United States." Again in 1783 Congress asked for power to levy duties on imports for a period of twenty-five years to be collected by state officers. This, too, was refused by the states. During a period of five years, the only response that Congress received from its requisitions was the sum of $2,000,000. According to Robert Morris: "Talking to the states is like preaching to the dead." They would not themselves raise the money necessary to carry on the functions of a central government which was on the brink of default on loans. Morris warned the nation that its public credit was gone, but Congress paid no attention to him.

George Washington after Addressing the Dissatisfied Officers at Newburgh

Defection in the Army

In addition to the default on government loans, the national army had not been paid and was ready to be mustered out. For a time between 1781 and 1783 there was a constant danger that the army would turn upon the government, overthrow it, and set up some form of dictatorship. George Washington was still commander of the army. He had rendered a great service to his country by his part in the Revolution. However, he was to render an even greater service to America through his action in 1783 when officers of the army had committed themselves to overthrow the national government to set up a military dictatorship. Upon learning of the plans of these officers and the place where they were to convene, he went to the scene at Newburgh and there delivered an address which could well rank among America's great state papers. He spoke to this group of men who were already committed to a program of treason and left them in tears as he related to them in his dynamic and sincere manner the story of the common suffering they had gone through together to make the United States of America an independent nation. So forceful was that heartbreaking appeal that the United States was undoubtedly saved from anarchy or dictatorship.

Washington peacefully disbanded the army shortly thereafter. Aside from certificates bearing interest at six percent and equal to full pay for five years for each man disbanded, they returned to their homes without pay. Not until the new government under the Constitution had been launched did they receive their money.

Commerce

The Confederation was also faced with serious problems of commerce, which was in a state of confusion. England discriminated against the new nation. Congress was without power to retaliate by passing its own navigation acts. Appeal to the states for such power was flatly rejected. Trade with the British West Indies was restricted. Some states passed their own tariff laws against foreign goods. The states engaged in commercial wars with one another. When one state closed its ports to English goods, a neighboring state would open its ports, thus nullifying any attempts to bring England to terms.

Massachusetts, New Hampshire, and Rhode Island enacted state navigation acts which placed tonnage duties on foreign vessels, taxed the importation of foreign goods, and forbade the exportation of goods in foreign vessels. The state of Connecticut, on the other hand, opened her ports to British shipping.

New York taxed firewood from Connecticut and the food which came from New Jersey's farms. The merchants of Connecticut banded together and refused to sell any goods to New York for a period of a year. New Jersey placed a heavy tax on a lighthouse which New York had built on New Jersey land.

Barbary pirates engaged in depredations against American commerce. With this picture of calamity within and without constantly before its eyes, Congress was bound hand and foot, utterly unable to help. Trade nearly came to a standstill in 1786.

Diplomacy

In diplomacy, the Confederation also found its lot a particularly difficult one. A united front to the world no longer existed. Foreign countries did not know whether they were dealing with one country or thirteen. England continued to hold forts in the Northwest, and Congress could not protest because they could not enforce the obligations of the Treaty of 1783 requiring recognition

Shay's Rebellion

of the rights of English creditors in America. England refused to negotiate a commercial treaty. Spain, in control of the Mississippi River, would not negotiate. France had loaned considerable money and was in doubt as to whether it would be repaid.

Paper Money

In spite of the experiences of the Continental Congress with paper currency, the states now attempted to meet the problems of the economic depression by issuing currency. Paper money agitation seriously endangered the country. Able men like Washington, Madison, Knox, Morris, and Hamilton made desperate attempts to stop the paper-money craze. The paper-money forces had gained an upper hand in many of the states.

Crisis in Massachusetts

Massachusetts was heavily in debt. The state government alone had contracted a debt of $15,000,000. In addition, practically all

61

the cities had bonded themselves, and individuals had spent more than their incomes in buying luxuries. Farmers vociferously blamed city merchants for the price slump in agricultural products. Bankers were denounced for mortgage foreclosures. Heavy tax burdens led the farmers to cry out that the merchants and bankers were not bearing their just share of the burden. Severe depression in maritime commerce caused unemployment and economic strife. All in all, the crisis had reached the point where everyone was blaming someone for something.

Paper-money forces, under the leadership of Captain Shays, a veteran of the Revolution, easily convinced the distressed people of Massachusetts that paper money was their way out. The people throughout the state adopted resolutions demanding issuance of paper money, but the legislature voted them down. Under Shays' forces agitation grew apace. Property foreclosures were stopped, and the courts were forcibly closed. To combat Shays' Rebellion, the governor of Massachusetts called out the militia under General Benjamin Lincoln and succeeded in ending the uprising.

Insufficient Authority

Thinking men from the start had visualized the inadequacy of the Articles of Confederation. Chief among these men were George Washington, Robert Morris, James Madison, Alexander Hamilton, and General Knox. In a paper called "The Continentalist," Alexander Hamilton showed in 1780 that the existing Congress under the Articles of Confederation was not vested with enough power to carry on the government of the country. For that reason he urged that Congress immediately resume the status of a Continental Congress and then call a convention of the states to consider a union of all states under a sovereign government with complete and absolute power of enforcement. Concurring with the opinion of Hamilton, George Washington declared that Congress must be given the controlling power in any system of federal government and that its power must be so complete as to give it absolute control over all affairs of common concern to the states. Further national strength was voiced in 1781 by Madison, who, as chairman of a congressional committee, reported in favor of the adoption by the states of an additional article giving Congress power to compel the states to comply with their obligations under the Articles.

The Annapolis Meeting

Other committees of Congress, from time to time, reported on suggested changes but always without success. Disagreement between Maryland and Virginia over navigation rights of the Potomac River led Virginia's legislature in 1785 to suggest that commissioners from both states meet to discuss the matter with Washington. The result was the Alexandria Conference. The whole question of commerce was discussed. After consultation, a call was sent out for a meeting of commissioners from neighboring states at Annapolis the following year. New York, Delaware, Pennsylvania, New Jersey, and Virginia sent delegates. However, only the question of the state of the union was considered by these representatives because conditions, economically as well as socially and politically, were serious by the time the Annapolis meeting convened. It was determined that another attempt should be made to call together a meeting of all thirteen states for the next year at Philadelphia. Alexander Hamilton, a representative for New York, was given the task of securing consent of the Congress and writing the call.

In the call to the convention, Hamilton emphasized the necessity for changing the Articles of Confederation. The Congress of the Confed-

eration issued the call for the Constitutional Convention to meet in Philadelphia in 1787.

Accomplishments under Confederation

Regardless of the existent disorder and confusion, there were accomplishments under the Confederation. It was under the Articles that the question of western lands had been settled. Every state ceded to the government its rights to the western lands and thereby established the public domain of the United States. When the lands had been ceded to the government, the next question arose: "How shall the government control these lands?" Enactment of the famous Northwest Ordinance of 1787, which set forth for all time the policy of the government with regard to the West in various stages of American history, was the answer to that question. The experience gained under the Articles laid the foundation stone for the "more perfect union" under the Constitution. The country was given the opportunity to test itself as well as the structure of the government. From it the nation realized the necessity for a stronger government in order to promote tranquility and prosperity. So, by no means, were the Articles of Confederation a complete failure.

Fundamental objections to the Confederation were the lack of the powers to regulate commerce, to levy taxes, to coin money and provide a uniform currency, and to forbid a state from impairing the obligations of contracts. The critical period which followed the adoption of the Articles of Confederation convinced the leaders of the new nation that without these powers vested in the national government, economic revival and national prosperity would be handicapped. The Constitutional Convention met in Philadelphia to discuss and settle these questions.

With the Articles as the starting point and the state constitutions as models, with Magna Carta, Petition of Right, and Bill of Rights behind the colonial charters, and with the background of the philosophies of Locke, Montesquieu, and Blackstone, the Constitution of the United States was drafted and a confederation was converted into a federal state.

TOPICAL OUTLINE FOR STUDY

A. Formation of the Confederation
  1. Second Continental Congress and the war
  2. Difficulties in drafting the Articles
    (a) Representation
    (b) Revenues
    (c) Western lands
  3. Major delay in ratification of the Articles due to controversy over the western lands
B. Provisions of the Articles of Confederation
  1. Executive, legislative, and judicial powers all vested in Congress
  2. Powers of the Congress of the Confederation
C. Internal, Social, Economic, and Political Conditions Within the United States After the Revolution
  1. Financial problems
  2. Commercial problems
  3. Diplomatic problems
  4. Paper-money craze (Shays' Rebellion)
D. Attempts to Remedy the Articles of Confederation
  1. Proposed amendments to the Articles
  2. Alexandria Conference
  3. Annapolis Convention
E. Call for the Constitutional Convention in Philadelphia

QUESTIONS

1. Upon what legal status did the Second Continental Congress function?
2. How did the Second Continental Congress operate during the first five years of the Revolution?
3. Disagreement over what three fundamental points delayed the adoption of the Articles of Confederation?
4. What was the primary delaying factor in the ratification of the Articles and how was it settled?

5. What did Article II of the Articles have to say about the power of the states?
6. How many delegates was each state entitled to under the Articles, and how many votes had each state?
7. List the ten most important powers vested in the Congress of the Confederation.
8. What three provisions in the Articles of Confederation were later destined to be in the Constitution?
9. Upon what did the Confederation build?
10. What was the immediate economic result of the termination of the Revolution?
11. In what financial position did the United States find itself during the critical period?
12. Relate the history of the attempts of 1781 and 1783 to grant more fiscal power to the Confederation.
13. Discuss fully the three fundamental weaknesses of the Confederation.
14. What were the causes and consequences of Shays' Rebellion?
15. Name some of the men who realized the inadequacy of the Confederation. What did they do about it?
16. What was the Alexandria Conference? What did it achieve?
17. What was the Annapolis Convention, and what was its greatest achievement?
18. List the accomplishments of the government under the Articles of Confederation.
19. Summarize the fundamental weaknesses of the Articles of Confederation.

CHAPTER 6

The Constitutional Convention

Delegates to the Constitutional Convention were named by the legislatures of the several states, which determined the number sent to the conference. Rhode Island's legislature, being controlled by forces favorable to paper money and opposed to a strong central government, refused to send delegates. All other states were represented. Sixty-five delegates were appointed, but ten did not appear at the meeting. Of the fifty-five in actual attendance only thirty-nine signed the Constitution. More than half were graduates of institutions of higher learning such as Princeton, Yale, Harvard, Columbia, Pennsylvania, William and Mary, Edinburgh, Glasgow, and Oxford. Here assembled the leading lawyers, merchants, financiers, farmers, and political leaders of the country. The oldest member in attendance was Benjamin Franklin, eighty-one, and the youngest was Jonathan Dayton, twenty-seven. Thirty-five were above the age of forty, and twenty were under forty.

Comparatively speaking, this was a convention of young men. Many had seen service under fire in the Revolution. Sol Bloom in *The Story of the Constitution* said: "These men were almost without exception acquainted with public affairs: forty-six had been members of one or both of the houses of the colonial or state legislatures; ten attended State constitutional conventions; sixteen had been or were to be governors. In national affairs forty-two were delegates to the Continental Congress, eight were signers of the Declaration of Independence, six signers of the draft of the

Articles of Confederation, seven had attended the Annapolis Convention and three had been executive officers under the Congress. . . . The positions which these men had occupied or were later to fill are indicative of the regard in which they were held by their fellow citizens, and of their character and worth."

George Washington

George Washington came to the convention as a delegate from Virginia. He had led the country through the Revolution and kept alive the idea of union at a time when his fellow countrymen were in despair. In his ceaseless activity and work through correspondence with the leaders of other states the Convention had had its origin.

George Washington

Impressed with the necessity for the establishment of a stable government, Washington had written the following note to Madison in March of 1787: "My wish is that the Convention may adopt no temporizing expedients, but probe the defects of the Constitution to the bottom and provide a radical cure, whether agreed to or not. A conduct of this kind will stamp wisdom and dignity on their proceedings, and hold up a light which sooner or later will have its influence."

His great contribution to the Convention was in acting as its presiding officer. Firmly and honestly, without fear or favor, he remained at the helm of the turbulent Convention through its ninety-nine days of hard work. Most fitting it was that in recognition of his service to the nation, he became the first President of the United States under the Constitution.

Benjamin Franklin

Pennsylvania sent its governor, then called president, Benjamin Franklin. He was probably the best known man in the Convention. Long before many of his colleagues had been born, he had been in the public service as a member of the Pennsylvania legislature, as postmaster general of the colonies, as a colonial agent in England, as a member of the Albany Congress of 1754, and the Continental Congress. As Minister to France during the Revolution, Franklin had a record which no other member of the Convention could approach except Washington. America was fortunate indeed that Providence should have spared this man to participate in the Constitutional Convention to help form a more perfect union, a union such as he envisioned as early as 1754 in the Albany Congress. Feeble with gout and age, this grand old man of the Convention effectively dignified it with his "homespun" philosophy of government. On one occasion his appeal saved the Convention from disruption.

James Madison

James Madison

The "Father of the Constitution" was James Madison of Virginia. From his early youth, Madison had made a deep study of all forms of government in the history of the world. His grasp of English history and constitutional law stamped him as a man with a deep knowledge of government. This was acknowledged by all members of the Convention. He contributed liberally from this store of knowledge, and though only thirty-six years of age, he had had a long career of public service. William Pierce, a delegate from Georgia, tells us that: "In the management of every great question he evidently took the lead in the Convention, and tho' he cannot be called an orator, he is a most agreeable,

69

Edmund Randolph

eloquent, and convincing Speaker." Intelligence, industry, honesty, and an amiable disposition made him beloved by his fellow delegates and gave him a position of leadership in the Convention. As the author of the Large State Plan, he was the father of the Constitution.

To Madison we are indebted for most of what little we know of the deliberations of the Convention, the sessions of which were secret. The most complete report of the proceedings were the notes which Madison carefully made day by day as the delegates labored on. These notes were not published until after his death. They constitute one of the primary sources of our knowledge of what happened on the floor of the Convention.

Edmund Randolph

One of Madison's fellow delegates was Governor Edmund Randolph of Virginia, a striking personality who had remained loyal to the American cause after his father had joined the loyalists. Randolph spoke with great eloquence and reasoning. In 1776 he had been a member of the convention which drafted the Virginia Constitution and Bill of Rights. At twenty-three he became Virginia's first state attorney general. He served as a delegate to the Continental Congress in 1779 and became governor of Virginia in 1786. His was the responsibility of presenting to the Convention a draft of a constitution prepared by Madison and known as the Virginia, or large-state, Plan. Randolph refused to sign the Constitution but worked for its ratification in Virginia.

Roger Sherman

Roger Sherman, who had started life as a shoemaker and had advanced to public positions in Connecticut, was noted for his common sense and honesty of purpose. His record as a state judge had been good, and his career in the state legislature and in the Continental Congress was filled with distinction. He played an important part in the Constitutional Convention and was instrumental in Connecticut's ratification of the Constitution.

Wilson of Pennsylvania

Probably the most learned man of the Convention was James Wilson of Pennsylvania. He had been educated in law in Scotland and possessed an extensive knowledge of legal institutions. He had studied in detail every revolution in world history down to his time. Fluent in speech, he participated in debate on all phases of the Constitution. He played an important part in framing its judicial clauses. He rallied support for ratification of the Constitution in the Pennsylvania Ratifying Convention.

Gouverneur Morris

Gouverneur Morris represented Pennsylvania. He was the Chairman of the Convention Committee on style and was responsible for the wording of the Constitution. A great orator and a fluent debater, his knowledge of rhetoric equipped him for his task. A lawyer by profession, he had turned merchant. Owing to his active interest in banking and commerce, he had served in Congress and had been the assistant superintendent of finance under the Confederation. He originated the American decimal system and was one of the first to foresee the value of the Erie Canal. With a charming personality and a nimbleness of wit, he fought for a strong national government.

Rufus King

From Massachusetts came Rufus King, recognized as a brilliant young man. William Pierce of Georgia described him: "This Gentleman is about thirty-three years of age, about five feet ten inches high, well formed, a handsome face, with a strong expressive eye, and a sweet high-toned voice." How the hearts of the Philadelphia belles must have fluttered at the sight of this man! Clearly seeing the dangers facing the country, he ably aided Madison in the fight to establish a national government. Sometimes rude in debate, he was a convincing speaker.

Rutledge of South Carolina

John Rutledge was South Carolina's leading public man. As a member of the Stamp Act and Continental Congresses, he was regarded as South Carolina's leading exponent of the colonial cause. During the war he was governor of that state. The legislature gave him powers of a dictatorial nature, so highly trusted was he by his people. He vigorously fought restrictions on the slave trade and was one of the leading advocates of the election of the President by Congress. Also from South Carolina was Charles Pinckney, who was a deep student of philosophy, law, and history. This gallant young man submitted a proposed plan of union which was considered by the Convention. His experience as a member of Congress had convinced him of the necessity for strong government.

Gouverneur Morris

Ellsworth, Mason, and Gerry

Honored for his ability and respected for his honesty was Oliver Ellsworth, a supreme court justice of Connecticut. Eloquent and effective in debate, his knowledge of governmental questions was clear. He had won fame for himself as a lawyer of great accomplishment.

One of the largest landowners of the country was George Mason of Virginia, who had drafted Virginia's famed Bill of Rights of 1776. It was his convincing logic that made it clear to the Convention that the new government must operate directly upon the people. He would not sign the Constitution because he feared the judicial and treaty making powers and because he believed that the Constitution should include a bill of rights. His fight on this point resulted in the adoption of the first ten amendments to our Constitution.

Another man who played a prominent part in the debates of the Convention, but refused to sign, was Elbridge Gerry of Massachusetts. He had been a member of Congress and was very prominent in local politics. Being a merchant, the lack of power to regulate commerce in the Confederation had convinced him of the necessity of a stronger form of government. Hesitant in speech, he took prominent part in debates but refused to sign the Constitution because he feared civil war in Massachusetts.

Alexander Hamilton

Alexander Hamilton was one of the delegates from New York. He had served through a good part of the Revolution as Washington's chief aide. Serving in Congress, he knew its weaknesses and he had become an inde-

Alexander Hamilton

fatigable advocate of a strong national government. The naming of two colleagues from New York who were very much opposed to any change in the Confederation placed Hamilton in an embarrassing position because he was in the minority. His contribution to the Convention, therefore, was not so great as it might have been. His plan of government, which he took five hours to explain, would have set up an extremely centralized national government. Young and enthusiastic, he was out of patience with "feeble government." Although the Constitution did not meet his hopes, he signed the document and undertook an aggressive and monumental fight in its behalf. With the aid of Madison and Jay, he penned the greatest exposition on government that has ever been written in this country, *The Federalist Papers*. Possessed of great personal magnetism, he was a convincing speaker. It was his logic that won New York's ratification of the Constitution.

Paterson, Morris, Johnson, and Wythe

The leader of the small-state group came from New Jersey, William Paterson, a lawyer of excellent ability. He had served in the Continental Congresses. A modest though fiery orator, he presented the New Jersey, or small-state, Plan to the Convention.

Robert Morris, the financier of the Revolution, was one of Pennsylvania's delegates. Outside of placing Washington in nomination as president of the Convention, Morris took practically no part in the debates of the Convention. He was probably the biggest businessman in the country. His commercial interests were national in scope, and as the superintendent of finance, he knew only too well the necessity for a strong and adequate national government with power to tax. Morris was the delegate who was closest to Washington during the sessions of the Convention.

From Connecticut came William Samuel Johnson, a Doctor of Laws from Oxford. He had been a member of Congress and fully comprehended the situation facing the nation. Having been a judge of the State Supreme Court, he was well grounded in law and the classics. His reputation as a scholar was continental. He later became President of Columbia College.

George Wythe—the law teacher of John Marshall, James Madison, and Thomas Jefferson—was in attendance as a delegate from Virginia. He shared with James Wilson a reputation for high legal attainment. His part in the Convention was the chairmanship of the committee on rules. His unreserved support of the Constitution, in the Virginia Ratifying Convention of 1788, made possible Virginia's ratification. Other men of lesser renown were present, no less earnest, no less honest, no less industrious, contributing what they had to offer. On horseback, they came hundreds of miles, leaving farms, businesses, and professions in order to contribute unselfishly of their energies to the creation of a more stable government. Respected for their personal qualities, these men were a fair sample of the caliber of leadership of the country in that day. With differing ideas of the remedies that should be applied, they came together. Out of the caldron of debate they molded the federal Constitution of the United States.

The Convention

The first order of business before the Convention, gathered at Independence Hall in Philadelphia, was the election of a presiding officer. At its first session of May 25, 1787, Robert Morris of Pennsylvania placed into nomination the name of George Washington for president of the Convention. The motion was seconded by John Rutledge of South Carolina. Unanimously elected, Washington was conducted to the chair by delegates Morris and Rutledge. Madison tells us that Washington "thanked the Convention for the honor they had conferred on him; reminded them of the novelty of the scene of business in which he was to act, lamented his want of better qualifications and claimed the indulgence of the House towards the involuntary errors which his inexperience might occasion." Major William Jackson was named secretary, and a committee was appointed to present the rules of the Convention. Each state was given one vote in the Convention, and seven states constituted a quorum. A majority of the states could prevail on any question, and it would be binding on the rest of the states. It is interesting to note that the Convention adopted the following rule: "Every member, rising to speak, shall address the President; and, while he shall be speaking, none shall pass between him, or hold discourse with another, or read a book, pamphlet, or paper, printed or manuscript."

Secret Proceedings

A rule was adopted to lock the doors of the Convention and provide for secrecy of its proceedings. The rule provided "that no copy be taken of any entry on the Journal during the sitting of the House, without leave of the House. That members only be permitted to inspect the Journal. That nothing spoken in the House be printed, or otherwise published, or communicated without leave."

The framers could see their only hope of successful execution of their task through secret proceedings. Men could give and take in debate without fearing any consequences from their constituents. Reaction from the public on deliberations were thus successfully forestalled until the Constitution was drafted. It speaks well of the character of these men to know that not one violated the rule and that the world had to wait for a half century until the death of Madison before his *Journal* told the story of the Convention.

The Fight for Ratification

On September 17, 1787, the Convention completed its work and the delegates affixed their signatures to the Constitution. James Madison reported that: "Whilst the last members were signing, Doctor Franklin, looking towards the President's chair, at the back of which a rising sun happened to be painted, observed to

Benjamin Franklin

a few members near him, that painters had found it difficult to distinguish in their art, a rising, from a setting, sun. I have, said he, often and often, in the course of the session, and the vicissitudes of my hopes and fears as to its issue, looked at that behind the President, without being able to tell whether it was rising or setting: but now at length, I have the happiness to know that it is a rising, and not a setting sun."

The Constitution was transmitted to the Congress of the Confederation, which in turn submitted it for ratification by conventions in the several states. At first it appeared that ratification was to be an easy matter, but before the battle was over, it became an arduous and tense affair.

Sixteen of the delegates to the Convention had not signed the Constitution, and most of these were now opponents of ratification. In New York, the delegates Lansing and Yates backed by Governor Clinton; in Maryland, the delegate Martin; in Massachusetts, the delegate Gerry; and in Virginia, the delegate Mason, aided by Richard Henry Lee, Patrick Henry, and James Monroe, created formidable opposition. In addition, there were men like Samuel Adams, John Hancock, and Edmund Randolph who were at first opposed but who were later won over to the cause of ratification for one reason or another.

Fortunately the friends of the Constitution were full of energy, arguments, and zeal. They employed every publicity medium of their day—newspapers, handbills, correspondence, pulpit, country store, pamphlets, and speeches. Alexander Hamilton, John Jay, and James Madison collaborated in writing *The Federalist Papers.* This series of essays remains to this day the ablest exposition and defense of the American Constitution which has ever been written. Washington, through correspondence with his friends, played an important part in the battle. The fact that he vigorously and enthusiastically favored the Constitution broke down a good part of the opposition, for the people had faith in his word.

Perhaps the most concise and typical criticism of the Constitution was best expressed by Elbridge Gerry of Massachusetts in a letter which he transmitted to the Massachusetts State Legislature. Said he: "My principal objections to the plan are, that there is no adequate provision for a representation of the people; that they have no security for the right of election; that some of the powers of the legislature are ambiguous, and others indefinite and dangerous; that the executive is blended with, and will have an undue influence over, the legislature; that the judicial department will be oppressive; that treaties of the highest importance may be formed by the President, with the advice of two thirds of a quorum of the Senate; and that the system is without the security of a bill of rights. These are objections which are not local, but apply equally to all the states." (Jonathan Elliott, *The Debates in the Several State Conventions on the Adoption of the Federal Constitution,* I, 1907 Edition, page 493.)

The first five ratifications came easily and by good majorities. Delaware was first to ratify on December 7, 1787, with a unanimous vote of its thirty delegates in the State Convention. On December 12, 1787, Pennsylvania ratified by a vote of 46 to 23. Then came two states with unanimous votes: New Jersey on December 18, 1787, and Georgia on January 2, 1788. Connecticut ratified on January 9, 1788, by a vote of 128 to 40. On February 6, 1788, Massachusetts joined the procession by a vote of 187 to 168. No other state ratified until April 28, 1788, when Maryland adopted the Constitution by a vote of 63 to 11. South Carolina followed on May 23, 1788, by a vote of 149 to 73. New Hampshire "joined the band" on June 21, by a vote of 57 to 47—a slim margin of 10 votes. The requisite nine states had now ratified and the Constitution would go into operation.

However, the eyes of the nation were on Virginia and New York, where the state conventions had been locked in desperate debate. Everyone knew that without them there could be no effective union of the states. Through the tireless efforts of James Madison, John Marshall, George Nicholas, and Edmund Randolph, Virginia joined the Union on June 26, 1788, by a vote of 57 to 47. The Herculean labors of Alexander Hamilton, John Jay, and Robert Livingston brought ratification from New York on July 26, 1788, by a vote of 30 to 27—a narrow margin of 3 votes. North Carolina's Convention adjourned in August 1788, without ratifying, but the North Carolinians changed their minds and ratified on November 21, 1789, by a vote of 194 to 77. Rhode Island did not even call a convention, but when it realized that the Union would go on without it and that Rhode Island ran the danger of being treated as a foreign country, it called a State Convention and by a vote of 34 to 32 finally ratified on May 29, 1790.

The ratification of the Constitution gave cause for great rejoicing throughout the land. Celebrations were held in cities like Philadelphia and New York.

In four months of hard work, the framers had produced a document which was destined to safeguard the greatest amount of liberty to the greatest number of people in the country. It was to secure the blessing of liberty to their posterity and, at the same time, to preserve the independence and the nationality of the United States of America.

TOPICAL OUTLINE FOR STUDY

A. Personnel of the Constitutional Convention
  1. How chosen
  2. Number
  3. Composition of the Convention
  4. Age of the members
  5. Leading members and states represented
    (a) Washington, Virginia
    (b) Madison, Virginia

      (c) Benjamin Franklin, Pennsylvania
      (d) Edmund Randolph, Virginia
      (e) Roger Sherman, Connecticut
      (f) James Wilson, Pennsylvania
      (g) Gouverneur Morris, Pennsylvania
      (h) Rufus King, Massachusetts
      (i) John Rutledge, South Carolina
      (j) Charles Pinckney, South Carolina
      (k) Oliver Ellsworth, Connecticut
      (l) George Mason, Virginia
      (m) Elbridge Gerry, Massachusetts
      (n) Alexander Hamilton, New York
      (o) William Paterson, New Jersey
      (p) Robert Morris, Pennsylvania

B. Rule of Procedure of the Convention
   1. Election of the officers
   2. Quorum
   3. Each state had one vote
   4. Secrecy

C. Ratification
   1. Opponents
   2. Proponents
   3. Main arguments against ratification
   4. Ratification by the state conventions

QUESTIONS

1. How were the delegates to the Constitutional Convention named?
2. Which of the states failed to send any delegates to the Convention? Why?
3. How many delegates were appointed? How many went to the Convention? How many signed the Constitution?
4. How many of the delegates were college men and in what institutions had they studied?
5. What was the age group of the members of the Convention?
6. What record of public service did these men have?
7. Name ten of the leading men in the Constitutional Convention and the contributions made by each.
8. Why was Madison called the "Father of the Constitution"?

9. Who was the President of the Convention?
10. What rules of procedure did the Convention adopt?
11. What did Franklin say when he signed the Constitution?
12. What were the main arguments used to fight ratification of the Constitution?
13. Who were some of the men who opposed the Constitution?
14. Who were some of the men who fought for ratification of the Constitution?
15. What were *The Federalist Papers* and who authored them?
16. How many states ratified the Constitution in 1787?
17. What states ratified in 1788?
18. When did Rhode Island and North Carolina ratify?

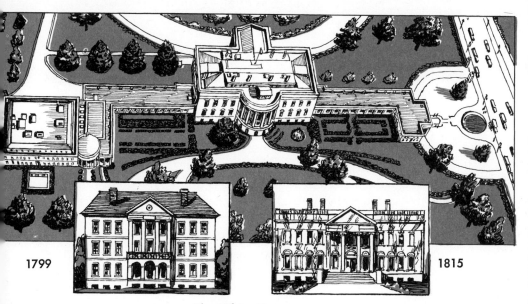

The White House

CHAPTER **7**

The Principles of the Constitution

Any study of the debates of the Convention, and of the Constitution itself, will clearly show that the framers sought to promote the "happiness" of the country through a form of government which would, insofar as humanly possible, guarantee and protect individual and political liberty.

These men did not regard the Constitution as perfect. They regarded it as the best set of principles to which they were all able to agree. Being not only idealists but also men of practical affairs, they felt that under the Constitution the nation could go forward in its path of progress and still preserve the institution of human liberty.

There are eight basic principles of government established by the Constitution. Each serves a specific purpose. The first of these is the principle of separation of powers.

Separation of Powers

Separation of the departments of government had, through the development of colonial and state governing institutions, come to be regarded as essential to the preservation of freedom. Congress was to legislate. The judiciary was to define the law. The executive was to give execution to the powers of government.

Practical experience had taught the fathers of the Constitution that each department of government could not exist rigidly independent of the others. Therefore, they developed a system of checks and balances whereby each department of government served as a check against the others. The President checks the Congress through his power to veto. Congress checks the President through the power to override his veto by a two-thirds vote, by the senatorial power to ratify appointments and treaties, and by the power of the House of Representatives to originate money bills. Over both, the courts of the country serve as a check through their power to evaluate the constitutionality of their actions.

Effectiveness of every other principle of the Constitution depends upon the maintenance and the observance of this separation of powers. Its purpose was very plainly stated by Madison when he said: "In framing a government which is to be administered by men over men the great difficulty lies in this: You must first enable the government to control the governed and in the next place oblige it to control itself."

Legislative Powers

In setting up the legislative branch of the Federal Government, the framers of the Constitution encountered wide divergence of opinion with regard to its composition, method of election, and tenure of office. The Convention established a two-house national legislature. One was known as the House of Representatives and the other as the Senate. The House was to be elected by the people. The Senate was to be selected by the several state legislatures. (The Seventeenth Amendment changed the election of Senators to popular election.) Representation of the several states in the

House was to be on the basis of population. In the Senate it was to be equal, two Senators from each state. Not only did they believe that the creation of the Senate was necessary in order to give constitutional recognition to the sovereignty of the states through equal representation in the Senate, but also they regarded the Senate as an actual check against the House of Representatives. Therefore, the House, as representative of the people, would be checked by the Senate, the representative of the states. By requiring two legislative bodies to agree in the enactment of legislation, the people would obtain a double check. Thus were the safeguards against hasty and ill-considered legislation set into operation.

The powers vested in Congress were delegated powers specifically set forth in the Constitution or reasonably implied therein. The "elastic clause" of the Constitution (Article I, Section 8, Clause 18) has served to confer upon Congress not only the specific powers delegated to it but also such additional powers as may be fairly or reasonably implied. This clause has played an important part in the way in which our government has developed.

Executive Powers

The executive powers under the Constitution are vested in the President of the United States. The high level to which the framers aspired in providing the method of electing the President is clearly shown by Hamilton in *The Federalist Papers:* "The process of election affords a moral certainty that the office of President will never fall to the lot of any man who is not in an eminent degree endowed with the requisite qualifications. Talents for low intrigue and the little arts of popularity may alone suffice to elevate a man to the first honors in a single state; but it will require other talents and a different kind of merit to establish him in the esteem and

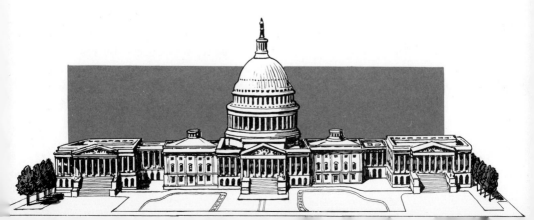

confidence of the whole Union, or in so considerable a portion of it as would be necessary to make him a successful candidate for the distinguished office of President of the United States."

Absence of an executive under the Articles of Confederation had forcefully demonstrated the necessity for this office. Therefore, the framers in conferring power on the President created a powerful executive. His duty is to see to the faithful execution of the laws. This means that the President has the power to call out the armed forces of the United States if he deems it necessary to execute the laws. The courts have liberally interpreted this power of the President and upheld him in practically any action if enforcement of law was the basis of his acts. From time to time under this clause the President issues executive orders filling in the detail of legislation when Congress so empowers him. This power alone would make the President an important officer of the government.

The Convention, recognizing the President as the chief officer of the nation, made him commander in chief of the army, navy, and militia. Control over the armed forces was checked by providing that Congress could not appropriate money for the armed forces for a greater period than two years. The power to wage war was not placed in his hands but in the hands of Congress. Power to negotiate treaties subject to ratification by the Senate enables the President to make peace and carry on the diplomatic affairs of the country. Authority to convene Congress into extra session is another of the President's powers. He also transmits information on the state of the union and recommendations for legislation to Congress. He can grant pardons to offenders against laws of the United States. With the advice and consent of the Senate, he appoints nonelected officers of the United States. The President may require in writing the opinion of "the principal Officer in each of the executive Departments."

He exercises a "qualified veto" over laws passed by Congress: his veto may be overridden by a two-thirds vote of both houses of Congress. The framers of the Constitution regarded this presidential power as an effective check against Congress. By reason of these constitutional powers, the President exercises a great practical control over the affairs of the nation, even though his powers are subject to checks and balances, including his being subject to removal by impeachment.

First Meeting Place of the Supreme Court

Judicial Powers

Careful attention was given by the many lawyers of the Convention to the definition of the powers vested in the judicial department of the government. The lack of a national judiciary to deal with interstate disputes under the Articles had been a great weakness. The framers were unanimously in favor of correcting this by creating a federal judicial system. The founders of the republic regarded this department as the weakest of the three.

The judiciary was given power over all cases involving the Constitution, national laws, and treaties. Cases involving citizens of different states, controversies between states, and states suing citizens of another state are tried in the federal courts. When the United States is a party to a suit, or there is a case involving admiralty and maritime matters, only the federal courts can try it.

The Constitution established the Supreme Court and gave Congress power to create courts inferior to the Supreme Court. Justices are appointed by the President with the advice and consent of the Senate. Tenure of justices was made for life because the framers believed that periodic appointments would be fatal to the independence of the judiciary. All federal courts except the Supreme Court are created by Congress and can be abolished by Congress. The number of federal judges is determined by Congress, including the number of justices on the Supreme Court. Congress defines the jurisdiction of all federal courts except the Supreme Court. *Neither the Congress nor the executive can deprive the courts of their judicial powers.*

Original jurisdiction is conferred by the Constitution on the Supreme Court in the following cases: "affecting Ambassadors, other public Ministers and Consuls, and those in which a State shall be Party." In all other cases, it has jurisdiction only by appeal from a lower federal court.

Trial by jury in the state in which the crime was committed was guaranteed by the judicial clauses of the Constitution.

Dual Form of Government

The second principle of the Constitution is the dual form of government, a national government sovereign in its sphere and the state governments sovereign in their spheres. Here was the origin of states' rights. This problem was one of the greatest constitutional problems which faced the Convention. The debates of the Convention clearly showed the fear of centralized government. At the same time it demonstrated that the delegates were seeking to better the situation that had prevailed under the Articles. They conferred on the national government all the powers necessary to make it an effective government. To the states were reserved all those powers which had not been delegated to the national government. Under this system the citizens of the states elect their local and state officers who legislate, administer, and adjudicate the laws of the state. At the same time the Federal Government protects them from foreign invasions, maintains the army and navy, regulates foreign and interstate commerce, and carries on other federal functions for their benefit.

Thus the framers of the Constitution preserved the state as an integral part of the union with sovereign authority over its people in the exercise of state functions. This is clearly realized when we note that the framers provided that the presidential electors should be chosen in a manner prescribed by the states. Equal representation was given to each state in the Senate, and the Senators were to be elected by the state legislators. A provision was written into the Constitution that no state could ever be denied its right to equal representation in the Senate without its own consent. The method of electing congressmen by the people was to be prescribed by the states. Thus, dependency on the state for election to office was established. Amendments to the Constitution were made possible only through action by state conventions or state legislatures or through state demand on Congress for the calling of a convention to submit amendments. Congress was prohibited from taxing the exports of states and giving preference to the ports of one state over those of another state. The states were prohibited by the Constitution from forming treaties or alliances, granting letters of marque, coining money, emitting bills of credit, making anything but gold or silver coin legal tender, passing bills of attainder, passing *ex post facto* laws, or any law impairing the obligations of a contract.

In effect, the framers denied to the states the exercise of any powers which would interfere with the efficient functioning of the Federal Government within its sphere. This denial of power was based upon experiences under the Articles of Confederation. For example, the states were prohibited from levying imposts or duties on imports and exports.

In order to protect a state from dismemberment the framers provided that new states cannot be formed from the territories of an existing state without the consent of that state's legislature and the approval of Congress.

A republican form of government is guaranteed to each state, and the Constitution declares that the Federal Government must protect each state from foreign invasion and from internal violence, such as riots.

Delegates of the Constitutional Convention were trying to strengthen the states by creating a central government which was dependent on the states. Without the states, there could be no United States. To further safeguard the states, the Tenth Amendment was added, reserving to the states all the powers not delegated to the national government nor prohibited to the states. By a careful and meticulous definition and prohibition of govern-

ing powers, the framers of the Constitution had successfully limited the powers of state and national government and created an "Indestructible Union of indestructible states."

Limited Powers

The third principle of our constitutional system is the doctrine of *limited powers*. We have already noted how the feeling had grown during colonial times that it was necessary to limit the powers of government in order to preserve liberty. Provision was made that the national government could exercise only those powers directly delegated to it and implied from this delegation. Both national and state governments were prohibited from passing *ex post facto* laws, bills of attainder, granting titles of nobility, and depriving a person of life, liberty, and property without the due process of law. The privilege of the writ of *habeas corpus* cannot be suspended in peacetime. Here the framers were seeking to protect all future Americans from arbitrary arrest and imprisonment as had occurred in England under Charles I and James II. Congress could not appropriate money for the support of armies for a longer term than two years. This was to protect the people from arbitrary government by compelling the President to go to Congress for the money necessary to maintain the army. The adoption of the first ten amendments after the ratification of the Constitution still further limited the power of the national government by guaranteeing personal liberty from encroachment by the Federal Government. This principle of limited government is an important one because the fathers of our Constitution feared governmental tyranny and were seeking protection for political liberty by its establishment.

Chief
Justice
Marshall

National Law Supreme

The *supremacy of national law* is the fourth constitutional principle. Within the sphere of its governmental purpose, the Federal Government is supreme. No state can pass a law contrary to the Constitution or in conflict with federal law.

Absence of such a provision in the Articles of Confederation had made the states supreme over the central government. So important did John Marshall regard this constitutional provision in a federal government that he said: "This principle is a part of the Constitution; and if there be any who deny its necessity, none can deny its authority."

Judicial Supremacy

The fifth principle of the Constitution is the doctrine of *judicial supremacy* or the right of the United States Supreme Court to pass upon the constitutionality of the actions of government.

Although the framers of the Constitution did not express themselves either in the debates of the Convention or in the Constitution itself with regard to this principle, their historic tradition shows that they were acquainted with the invalidation of acts of their colonial assemblies. Also, they were familiar with cases where state courts had declared acts of state legislatures unconstitutional.

Hamilton, in arguing for the ratification of the Constitution and in explaining the judicial clauses, clearly set forth the argument that a government of limited powers could function only under a written constitution, provided some part of the government had the right to determine when the limits of the constitution had been transgressed.

What department of government should exercise the power? It is obvious to everyone that the power cannot be vested in the executive branch of the government. If such were the case, then the executive could determine the constitutionality of his own acts and would unite in the hands of the physical and military power of the nation the determination of the purposes to which this power might be put. This would be a *denial of government by law*. Hence, the power to pass upon the constitutionality of the actions of government could only be placed in the legislative or judicial branches of the government. It would have been dangerous to repose it in Congress because then Congress would become the judge of its own actions. Its structure is such that its membership could be swayed by prejudice and not always respond to reason and logic or restrain its own freedom of action. Therefore, the power could not be vested in the legislative department of the government.

The only other place in which the power could be vested was in the judicial department. By placing it there, the United States made a contribution to the political science of the world. This judicial supremacy is balanced by the fact that both the legislative and executive branches of the government possess powers with which the courts cannot interfere. Congress determines the policies of government under its broad limit of delegated powers. The judiciary cannot interfere with this field. It can only see that the powers do not exceed the constitutional limits. The courts are dependent upon the Congress for the appropriations of moneys needed for their operation. Congress defines their full jurisdiction, ordains and establishes inferior courts to the Supreme Court, and determines the number of judges, compensation, and such.

The courts can intervene only as against the President when he attempts to exercise a power not granted to him by the Constitution. As regards the powers actually granted by the Constitution, the President is free from judicial control. The courts must look to the executive in the last resort for the enforcement of their judgments and decrees.

In the first case in which the United States Supreme Court declared an act of Congress unconstitutional, in 1803, Chief Justice John Marshall set forth the reasons why the United States Supreme Court had such power. In this case Marshall set forth a major premise: that the courts of the land do two things—interpret and apply the laws. From this major premise he developed an able argument. The fundamental principle behind the American government lies in the limit placed on the powers of the various departments of the government. Constitutions are written in order that these limits may not be mistaken. What can be the purpose of these limits if those whom it intended to restrain surpass them? There can be no middle ground. Either the Constitution is the "superior paramount law not to be changed by legislative enactment," or otherwise it is merely on a level with legislative acts and as such can be altered by the will of Congress. If the Constitution is supreme, then an act of Congress contrary to the Constitution is not supreme. If the Constitution is not supreme, then written constitutions are "absurd attempts on the part of the people to limit a power in its own nature illimitable."

The Supreme Court cannot interpret the law or apply it without reference to the Constitution, which expressly states that the Constitution itself is part of the supreme law of the land. The whole theory of our Federal Government would be denied if the Supreme Court examined the laws of Congress in the light of common law only and not with the Constitution in view. Such an approach would be subversive of the written Constitution because *it* is the definer of the judicial power of the courts. It is the *rule of evidence* for the court. A bill to punish a person for a crime of which he has not been tried or an *ex post facto* bill cannot be made law. But suppose that Congress passes such laws, then whose duty is it to say that the laws violate the Constitution? This duty belongs to the courts because they must interpret and apply the law. The Constitution states that no person can be convicted of treason unless on the testimony of two witnesses to the same overt act or on confession in open court. The language of the Constitution is here clearly directed to the *court*. Constitutional principles then cannot yield to legislative acts.

From time to time throughout its history, the Supreme Court has rendered controversial decisions which have brought down upon it the criticism of many citizens and put the court under the "fire" of Congress and/or the President. For example, in 1937 President Roosevelt was so dissatisfied by the court's decisions that he attempted to "pack" the court.

Twenty years later, in 1957, as a result of a series of very highly controversial decisions, the federal courts came under the "fire" of Congress again. Senators and Congressmen from all over the nation have expressed concern that the United States Supreme Court was sacrificing state sovereignty to federal authority and rendering ineffective the legislation passed by Congress to combat communism in the nation.

President Eisenhower said that in the court's latest "series of decisions there are some that each of us has very great trouble understanding." He also said: "I think we should not forget this: The Supreme Court is just as essential to our system of Government as is the President or as is the Congress, and we should respect its duties and its responsibilities." (*Congressional Quarterly,* Number 27, page 807.)

Congressman Rivers of South Carolina recently said: "The Supreme Court has prostituted the organic law of this land and arrogated unto itself the legislative functions of the Congress. It has interpreted law that is not and written laws that should not be written." (*Congressional Record,* August 9, 1957, page A6494.)

On the other hand, Chairman Cellar of the House Judiciary Committee, a Congressman from New York, on July 1, 1957, said

Chief Justice Warren

to the *Congressional Quarterly:* "I will not countenance any kind of hocus-pocus legislation aimed at the Supreme Court. The Court has been attacked often before and has survived. It will survive this attack and those who are criticizing it now will have reason in the future to be glad it is still around."

Dozens of bills and constitutional amendments to reverse the Supreme Court and to circumscribe its powers were pending in the last (1959) session of Congress. All bills of this nature failed.

Congress can increase or decrease the number of justices of the Court. It has the power of confirmation and the power to impeach the justices. It can define the court's appellate jurisdiction. It can reverse the court's interpretation of the laws by enactment of new legislation, but the court's power to declare laws of Congress unconstitutional can only be changed by a constitutional amendment.

How to Change the Constitution

The sixth principle of the Constitution is the *amending process.* The difficulties incident to the attempted amendment of the Articles of Confederation had convinced the framers of the necessity of an amending process which would work when public opinion was sufficiently unanimous. Under the Articles of Confederation, unanimous consent of all states to an amendment had been necessary. On several occasions one state's refusal to ratify an amendment had made impossible any change in the Articles. It had been the failure to secure amendments to the Articles of Confederation which had made necessary the Constitutional Convention.

In order to make the amending process effective, two methods of initiating amendments are provided. Should Congress fail to submit an amendment, two-thirds of the states can demand a national constitutional convention for that purpose. The framers were seeking an amending process which, although effective, would not be too easy. The requirements for a two-thirds vote of both houses of Congress and ratification by three-fourths of the states was the result.

That they ably safeguarded the amending process from abuse is attested to by the fact that although several thousand amendments have been proposed in Congress, only twenty-seven were submitted to the states. Of these, only twenty-two were ratified between 1789 and 1953. Amendments to the Constitution can come only after long discussion and as the result of a persistent, widespread, national demand.

As long as the principle of the amending process is in the Constitution, there is *an orderly and legal method of adjusting the powers of government to the will of the people.*

Liberty

The seventh principle of the Constitution is *preservation of individual and political liberty*. This principle did not become well formed until after the adoption of the first ten amendments to the Constitution and will, therefore, be discussed at length under the chapter on the American Bill of Rights.

Representative Republican Government

The eighth principle of the Constitution established by the framers is a *representative republican government*. One of America's ablest jurists, Judge Cooley, has well stated the principle of republican government when he said: "A republican government is a government of representatives chosen by the people, as a contrast on one side with a democracy, in which the people or community as an organized whole wields its sovereign powers of government, and on the other, with the rule of one man, as king, emperor, czar, or sultan, or with that of one class of men, as an aristocracy. . . . By a 'republican form of government' was intended a government in which not only would the people's representatives make the laws and their agents administer them, but the people would also, directly or indirectly, choose the executive. *But it would by no means follow that the whole body of the peo-*

First Session of the United States Senate

ple, or even the whole body of adults or competent persons, would be admitted to political privileges; and in any republican state the law must determine the qualification for admission to the elective franchise." In a republic, political privileges are extended only to those who can meet the requirements. For that reason, everyone does not necessarily exercise the right to vote.

In pointing out the difference between a democracy and a republic, Madison said: "The two great points of difference between a democracy and a republic are: *first,* the delegation of the government in the latter, to a small number of citizens elected by the rest; *secondly,* the greater number of citizens in extended territory which may be brought within the compass of republican than of democratic government. . . . The effect of the first difference is, on the one hand, to refine and enlarge the public views, by passing them through the medium of a chosen body of citizens, whose wisdom may best discern the true interest of their country and whose patriotism and love of justice will be least likely to sacrifice it to temporary or partial consideration. . . . The true distinction between these forms is that in a democracy they meet and exercise the government first. In a republic they assemble and administer it by their representative agents."

The Constitution guarantees a republican form of government to every state in the union. When the Constitution of the United States went into operation, all the states in the union had state constitutions. The people of the states, through their elected representatives, had participated in the drafting of these constitutions. The governments that they set up were not changed by the federal Constitution. They were accepted as they were. The Supreme Court has ruled: "It is therefore to be presumed that they were such as it was the duty of the states to provide. Thus, we have unmistakable evidence of what was republican in form, within the meaning of that term as employed in the Constitution." The type of state government in existence in 1787 was therefore a "republican government."

Eight Basic Principles

Thus did the framers of the Constitution write eight basic principles into the American Constitution: first, separation of powers; second, dual government; third, limited powers; fourth, supremacy of national law; fifth, judicial supremacy; sixth, amending process; seventh, individual and political liberty; and eighth, republican government. With these principles, they formed "a more perfect Union," established "Justice," insured "domestic Tranquility," provided "for the common defence," promoted "the general Welfare," and secured "the Blessings of Liberty" to themselves and their posterity.

TOPICAL OUTLINE FOR STUDY

A. Separation of Powers
    1. System of checks and balances
    2. Checks on Congress
    3. Checks on the executive
    4. Checks on the judiciary
B. Dual Form of Government
    1. Division of power between the states and the federal government
    2. Place of the states in the Union
    3. "States' rights"
C. Limited Powers
    1. Limitations on the powers of the national government
    2. "Government of laws, not of men"
D. Supremacy of the National Law
    1. Supremacy in field of national government
    2. Supreme law of the land
E. Judicial Supremacy
    1. Judicial power
    2. Balanced "judicial supremacy"
    3. Constitutionality of federal legislation
    4. Problem today
F. Amending Process
    1. Two methods of initiating amendments
    2. Importance of the amending principle
G. Liberty
H. Representative Republican Government
    1. Government of a republic

2. Democracy
3. Importance of this principle

QUESTIONS

1. Did the authors of the Constitution regard it as perfect?
2. What are the eight principles of the Constitution?
3. Upon what does the effectiveness of the principles of the Constitution depend?
4. What are the safeguards in the Constitution against "hasty" and "ill-considered" legislation?
5. Why was the office of President created?
6. Of what importance is the presidential oath of office?
7. What is the importance of the Supreme Court in our form of government?
8. How do the state and national governments balance one another?
9. Why did the framers of the Constitution preserve the state as an integral part of the Union?
10. How did the Constitution establish a "limited" government?
11. Why was national law made supreme?
12. Upon what constitutional theory is the power of the Supreme Court based?
13. What constitutes the judicial power of the United States government?
14. In how many ways can amendments to the Constitution be initiated?
15. Describe the four methods by which the Constitution may be amended.
16. What did Madison say were the two great points of difference between a "republic" and a "democracy"?
17. What kind of government did the Constitution establish?
18. What debt do we owe to the framers of our Constitution?

CHAPTER **8**

The Constitution

PREAMBLE

We, the People of the United States, in Order to form a more perfect Union, establish Justice, insure domestic Tranquility, provide for the common defence, promote the general Welfare, and secure the Blessings of Liberty to ourselves and our Posterity, do ordain and establish this Constitution for the United States of America.

The preamble to the Constitution sets forth the objectives of the Federal Government. These are declared to be the formation of a more perfect union, the establishment of justice and domestic tranquility, the promotion of common defense and the general welfare, and the securing of the blessings of liberty. Although the preamble is not the source of any of the Federal Government's power, it does state the scope and purpose of the Constitution. The Constitution was ordained and established not by the states but by the people. This the preamble clearly sets forth in the words: "We, the People of the United States, . . . , do ordain and establish this Constitution for the United States of America."

Article I **THE CONGRESS**

Legislative Powers

SECTION 1

All legislative Powers herein granted shall be vested in a Congress of the United States, which shall consist of a Senate and House of Representatives.

On May 29, 1787, the Convention commenced its debate on the question of whether it would erect a strong national government or merely expand the powers of Congress under the Articles of Confederation. Governor Randolph presented the Virginia, or large-state, Plan, and Governor Paterson presented the New Jersey, or small-state, Plan. This debate revealed that there were two distinct groups in the Convention. Massachusetts, Pennsylvania, Virginia, North Carolina, South Carolina and Georgia formed the large-state party. They favored the creation of a real national government and opposed the equal representation of each state in Congress. On the other hand, Connecticut, New Jersey, Maryland, Delaware, and New York were members of the small-state party. They stood by the Articles of Confederation and advocated equal representation for each state in Congress.

For many days the Convention debated what the basis of representation was to be. Finally, Ellsworth of Connecticut suggested the establishment of a Congress of two houses with equal representation of the states in one and representation on the basis of population in the other. Benjamin Franklin supported Ellsworth's plan and suggested the appointment of a committee to work out a compromise.

This committee reported in favor of a bicameral national legislature, a House of Representatives to be chosen on a basis of population and a Senate in which representation was to be equal, with two Senators coming from each state. For eleven days the Convention debated the report and finally it was put to a vote. Six states favored the compromise and fives states opposed it. Thus, by a majority of one state, the Great Compromise of the Convention was adopted.

From this section of the Constitution flow two doctrines of

American constitutional law. The first is that our national government is one of delegated powers. The second is that Congress cannot delegate its legislative powers, for this section says that "All legislative Powers . . . shall be vested in the Congress of the United States." These powers belong to Congress and can only be exercised by Congress. If Congress could delegate these powers, then the principle of separation of powers would be destroyed. However, Congress may vest in executive officers the power to make rules and regulations for enforcement of a law.

The House of Representatives

SECTION 2

The House of Representatives shall be composed of Members chosen every second Year by the People of the several States, and the Electors in each State shall have the Qualifications requisite for Electors of the most numerous Branch of the State Legislature.

No person shall be a Representative who shall not have attained to the Age of twenty-five Years, and been seven Years a citizen of the United States, and who shall not, when elected, be an Inhabitant of that State in which he shall be chosen.

Representatives and direct Taxes shall be apportioned among the several States which may be included within this Union, according to their respective Numbers, which shall be determined by adding to the whole Number of free Persons, including those bound to Service for a Term of Years, and excluding Indians not taxed, three-fifths of all other Persons.* The actual Enumeration shall be made within three Years after the first Meeting of the Congress of the United States, and within every subsequent Term of ten Years, in such Manner as they shall by Law direct. The Number of Representatives shall not exceed one for every thirty Thousand, but each State shall have at Least one Representative; and until such enumeration shall be made, the State of New Hampshire shall be entitled to chuse three, Massachusetts eight, Rhode-Island and Providence Plantations one, Connecticut five, New-York six, New-Jersey four, Pennsylvania eight, Delaware one, Maryland six, Virginia ten, North Carolina five, South Carolina five, and Georgia three.

When vacancies happen in the Representation from any State, the

---

* Provisions of the Constitution that are no longer in effect or have been changed by amendments are overprinted with a blue line.

Executive Authority thereof shall issue Writs of Election to fill such Vacancies.

The House of Representatives shall chuse their Speaker and other Officers; and shall have the sole Power of Impeachment.

Representation of the several states in the House of Representatives is on the basis of population. Believing that the House should have an immediate dependence on—and be in sympathy with—the people, the framers of the Constitution felt that frequent elections were essential to the preservation of our liberty. Since representation was a substitute for a meeting of citizens in person, they believed that biennial elections to the House would tend to bring the national government into common interest with the people of the country.

In the Convention, the northern states sought to exclude slaves from being counted in determining representation in Congress. Southern states insisted on their being counted for representation but objected to any taxation on them. Someone directed the Convention's attention to an act passed in 1783 by the Congress of the Confederation apportioning supplies to the states for the common treasury on the whole number of free inhabitants and three-fifths of all other persons. By following this previous law, the Constitutional Convention adopted its second compromise providing that three-fifths of the Negro slaves should be counted in determining representation in Congress and for purposes of national taxation. Eleven states under the Confederation had approved this ratio, and the vote in the Convention was unanimous. The adoption of the Fourteenth and Sixteenth Amendments altered this compromise.

The second section of Article I of the Constitution provides for

1. Election of the House of Representatives (Congressmen) every two years by voters whose qualifications are defined by state law. The right of a citizen to vote for members of Congress has its foundation in the Constitution. Congress may protect this right by appropriate legislation. The Constitution declares that the same qualifications apply to those electing a Representative to Congress as the state demands of its citizens who vote for the members of the lower house of a state legislature.

2. Qualifications of Congressmen. The person must be at least twenty-five years of age, a citizen for at least seven years, and an inhabitant of the state from which elected.

3. Apportionment of Representatives in Congress and direct taxes. Under existing statute, Congress has provided for 435 members. The admission of Alaska and Hawaii adds two additional Representatives—one from each of these new states. The total number of Representatives will revert to 435 in 1960 unless Congress passes a statute increasing the number to 437. Since Congress may change the number of Representatives after each census, it is very possible that after the census of 1960 there will be a new reapportionment statute.

4. Filling of vacancies by special elections on the call of the governor of the state where the vacancy exists.

5. The House choosing its Speaker and other officers.

6. Vesting in the House the sole power of impeachment. By "impeachment" is meant that a public official is accused of misconduct in office. Article II, Section 4, of the Constitution lists the crimes for which a public official can be impeached. It is the duty of the House to make these accusations, acting similarly to a grand jury in that its members can decide if an official should be tried for a crime. The Senate tries all impeachment cases (Article I, Section 3, Clause 6).

The Senate

SECTION 3

The Senate of the United States shall be composed of two Senators from each State, chosen by the Legislature thereof, for six Years; and each Senator shall have one Vote.

Immediately after they shall be assembled in Consequence of the first Election, they shall be divided as equally as may be into three Classes. The Seats of the Senators of the first Class shall be vacated at the Expiration of the second Year, of the second Class at the Expiration of the fourth Year, and the third Class at the Expiration of the sixth Year, so that one third may be chosen every second Year; and if Vacancies happen by Resignation, or otherwise, during the Recess of the Legislature of any State, the Executive thereof may make temporary Appointments until the next Meeting of the Legislature, which shall then fill such Vacancies.

No person shall be a Senator who shall not have attained to the Age of thirty Years, and been nine Years a Citizen of the United States, and who shall not, when elected be an Inhabitant of that State for which he shall be chosen.

The Vice President of the United States shall be President of the Senate, but shall have no Vote, unless they be equally divided.

The Senate shall chuse their other Officers, and also a President pro tempore, in the Absence of the Vice President, or when he shall exercise the Office of President of the United States.

The Senate shall have the sole Power to try all Impeachments. When sitting for that Purpose, they shall be on Oath or Affirmation. When the President of the United States is tried, the Chief Justice shall preside: And no Person shall be convicted without the Concurrence of two thirds of the Members present.

Judgment in Cases of Impeachment shall not extend further than to removal from Office, and disqualification to hold and enjoy any Office of honor, Trust or Profit under the United States: but the Party convicted shall nevertheless be liable and subject to Indictment, Trial, Judgment and Punishment, according to Law.

The framers of the Constitution believed that the creation of the Senate was necessary in order to give constitutional recognition to the sovereignty of the states through equal representation in the Senate. They provided for two Senators from each state to be selected by the state legislatures. The adoption of the Seventeenth Amendment altered this by providing for popular election.

In order to give stability to the legislative branch of the national government, the framers provided a six-year term for members of the Senate. The terms of one-third of the Senators expire every two years. This makes the Senate a continuous body and assures an upper branch with experienced men well acquainted with the various problems of government.

The third section of Article I of the Constitution provides for

1. Election of two Senators by each state legislature for a term of six years. (The Seventeenth Amendment now provides for election by the people. In case of vacancies, it permits the state legislatures to authorize the governor to make a temporary appointment pending the holding of an election.)
2. One vote for each Senator.

3. Qualifications for Senators. The person must be at least thirty years of age, a citizen for at least nine years, and an inhabitant of the state from which elected.

4. The Vice President to be President of the Senate, without having a vote in that body except in case of a tie. As President of the Senate, the Vice President is in a unique position for being able to determine firsthand the feelings and points of view of the Senate on important legislative programs. He can act as a "reporter" for the President in keeping him in touch with current trends in the Senate. So important a role has this become that all three of the recent Vice Presidents came from the Senate—Truman, Barkley, and Nixon.

The Vice President can cast a vote to resolve a tie in the Senate. This right can be important to an administration if each party is almost equally represented in the Senate. In 1899, Vice President Hobart cast the vote which defeated independence for the Philippines. In 1959, Vice President Nixon cast the vote that added the McClellan "bill of rights" to the Kennedy Labor Reform Bill.

5. A President pro tempore and other officers to be elected by the Senate. By "pro tempore" is meant "for the time being." Thus, if the Vice President becomes the President of the United States upon the death of the elected President, or if the Vice President is absent from the Senate, the President pro tempore presides.

6. Trial of impeachments by the Senate. The Senate has the duty of deciding the guilt or innocence of those public officials who have been accused of crimes listed in Article II, Section 4. The Chief Justice of the United States, not the Vice President, presides over trials of impeachment in which the President of the United States is accused of a crime.

7. Two-thirds vote of Senate to convict and define judgment in cases of conviction of impeachment.

Elections

SECTION 4

The Times, Places, and Manner of holding Elections for Senators and Representatives, shall be prescribed in each State by the Legis-

lature thereof; but the Congress may at any time by Law make or alter such Regulations, except as to the Places of chusing Senators.

The Congress shall assemble at least once in every Year, ~~and such Meeting shall be on the first Monday in December, unless they shall by Law appoint a different Day.~~

The Constitution allows the states to determine the time of elections, all but Alaska and Hawaii (1959) having selected the Tuesday after the first Monday in November.

Congress can protect the voter from violence and from intimidation, and the election from fraud and corruption. Congress has the right to guarantee honest elections to the people. Congress requires that voting be by written ballot. It has also passed acts regulating campaign expenditures and forbidding certain political practices.

In our study of the historical background of the Constitution, we have seen how a despotic king or colonial governor could assemble and dismiss the representatives of the people according to his own needs and desires. In order to avoid such a condition the framers of the Constitution made it explicit that Congress should meet regularly so that the right of the people to govern themselves would be safeguarded.

This section was altered by the adoption of the Twentieth Amendment, which provided that Congress shall assemble at noon on the third of January in each year unless Congress by law sets a different day.

Rules and Procedures

SECTION 5

Each House shall be the Judge of the Elections, Returns and Qualifications of its own Members, and a Majority of each shall constitute a Quorum to do Business; but a smaller Number may adjourn from day to day, and may be authorized to compel the Attendance of absent Members, in such Manner, and under such Penalties as each House may provide.

Each House may determine the Rules of its Proceedings, punish its Members for disorderly Behaviour, and, with the Concurrence of two thirds, expel a Member.

Each House shall keep a Journal of its Proceedings, and from time

HOUSE OF REPRESENTATIVES
PRESIDING OFFICER: Speaker of the House
MEMBERSHIP: 437 Representatives, proportioned according to state population, directly elected by the people

to time publish the same, excepting such Parts as may in their Judgment require Secrecy; and the Yeas and Nays of the Members of either House on any question shall, at the Desire of one fifth of those Present, be entered on the Journal.

Neither House, during the Session of Congress, shall, without the Consent of the other, adjourn for more than three days, nor to any other Place than that in which the two Houses shall be sitting.

Section 5 of Article I provides for

1. Power to each House to judge elections and qualifications of its members. To protect our democracy, the Constitution grants to Congress the power to decide if a man elected Senator or Representative has fulfilled the qualifications for

SENATE
PRESIDING OFFICER: Vice President of the United States
MEMBERSHIP: 100 Senators, 2 from each state, directly elected by the people

his office and if he was honestly elected. The Senate and House each judge their own members.

2. Requiring a quorum consisting of a majority of each House in order to conduct official business. Quorum means more than a majority. With the admission of Alaska and Hawaii as states, a quorum becomes 51 in the Senate and 219 in the House. Even if there is not a quorum present, either House may adjourn from day to day and may under its rules compel the attendance of absent members.

3. Authority for each House to compel attendance of absent members.

4. Power to each House to adopt rules of procedure, punish members, and, by a two-thirds vote, expel members.

107

5. The keeping of a journal of proceedings by each House. (This journal is known as the *Congressional Record*. Prior to 1837 it was known as the *Register of Debates,* and from 1837 to 1873 it was called the *Congressional Globe.*

6. That neither House can adjourn without the consent of the other except for a period of three days.

Compensation and Privileges and Immunities

SECTION 6

The Senators and Representatives shall receive a Compensation for their Services, to be ascertained by Law and paid out of the Treasury of the United States. They shall in all Cases, except Treason, Felony, and Breach of the Peace, be privileged from Arrest during their Attendance at the Session of their respective Houses, and in going to and returning from the same; and for any Speech or Debate in either House, they shall not be questioned in any other Place.

No Senator or Representative shall, during the Time for which he was elected, be appointed to any civil Office under the Authority of the United States, which shall have been created, or the Emoluments whereof shall have been encreased during such time; and no Person holding any Office under the United States, shall be a member of either House during his Continuance in Office.

This section provides for

1. Compensation and immunities of members of both Houses. Members of Congress under the Confederation were paid by the states. It was felt by the Constitutional Convention that the salary of Senators and Representatives should come out of the treasury of the United States, thereby giving them a degree of independence from the states. The compensation of Senators and Representatives is $22,500 per annum plus a limited amount for expenses. The Speaker of the House and the Vice President of the United States receive $35,000 per annum.

   The privileges and immunities which this section accords to members of Congress are for the purpose of protecting the rights of the people by enabling the members of Congress to execute the functions and duties of their offices without fear.

2. Restrictions on members of Congress holding office under the United States. Members of Congress, during their elected terms, cannot be appointed to any civil office which has been created or the pay increased during the member's term of office in Congress. No person who holds an office under the United States can serve in Congress.

These rules were written into the Constitution in order to avoid those abuses that occurred many times under colonial governments, when the separation of powers was undermined by the governors (see page 24).

Procedure for Legislative Bills

SECTION 7

All Bills for raising Revenue shall originate in the House of Representatives; but the Senate may propose or concur with Amendments as on other Bills.

Every Bill which shall have passed the House of Representatives and the Senate, shall, before it become a Law, be presented to the President of the United States; if he approve he shall sign it, but if not he shall return it, with his Objections to that House in which it shall have originated, who shall enter the Objections at large on their Journal, and proceed to reconsider it. If after such Reconsideration two thirds of that House shall agree to pass the Bill, it shall be sent, together with the Objections, to the other House, by which it shall likewise be reconsidered, and if approved by two thirds of that House, it shall become a Law. But in all such Cases the Votes of both Houses shall be determined by Yeas and Nays, and the Names of the Persons voting for and against the Bill shall be entered on the Journal of each House respectively. If any Bill shall not be returned by the President within ten days (Sundays excepted) after it shall have been presented to him, the Same shall be a Law, in like Manner as if he had signed it, unless the Congress by their Adjournment prevent its Return, in which Case it shall not be a Law.

Every Order, Resolution, or Vote to which the Concurrence of the Senate and House of Representatives may be necessary (except on a question of Adjournment) shall be presented to the President of the United States; and before the Same shall take Effect, shall be approved by him, or being disapproved by him, shall be repassed by two thirds of the Senate and House of Representatives, according to the Rules and Limitations prescribed in the Case of a Bill.

This section does three important things. First, it provides that all bills for raising revenue shall originate in the House of Representatives. The framers were aware of the struggle between the colonial governor and the colonial legislature for the control of the purse strings. They felt that the House directly representing the people should have the sole power of initiating bills to levy taxes. Second, all bills passed by Congress must be submitted to the President for his action. The President can do several things about them:

1. He may sign the bill, in which case it becomes law.
2. He may refuse to sign it (veto). In this case, he returns the bill to the House of origin with the reason for his action. Any bill may be passed over the President's veto by a two-thirds vote of each House.

   Thus, the President does not have the absolute veto power over legislation which most colonial governors possessed (see page 24). The framers of the Constitution made certain that this control of the legislature by the executive did not find its way into the government of the United States.
3. If Congress is in session and the President fails to return the bill within ten days (Sundays excepted), the bill becomes a law without the President's signature.
4. If Congress adjourns within ten days (Sundays excepted) of the presentation of a bill to the President and he fails to act on it, the bill dies. This is called "pocket veto." If the President does not like the bill, "he can put it in his pocket and forget about it."

Third, the last clause of this section seeks to prohibit Congress from passing legislation and circumventing the President by calling it a resolution, order, or vote. By precedent this has come to mean that any "Order, Resolution or Vote" having *the force of law* must be submitted to the President for his approval. Resolutions of Congress proposing amendments to the Constitution need not be approved by the President. Nor are concurrent resolutions subject to presidential approval. During World War II, legislation passed to meet the wartime emergency contained provisions to the effect that Congress could terminate the legislation by means of a concurrent resolution, thus ending the President's power without his concurrence. Examples of this were the Emergency Price Control Act of 1942 and the War Labor Disputes Act of 1943.

Powers of Congress

SECTION 8

The Congress shall have Power to lay and collect Taxes, Duties, Imposts and Excises, to pay the Debts and provide for the common Defence and General Welfare of the United States; but all Duties, Imposts and Excises shall be uniform throughout the United States;

To borrow Money on the credit of the United States;

To regulate Commerce with foreign Nations, and among the several States, and with the Indian Tribes;

To establish an uniform Rule of Naturalization, and uniform Laws on the subject of Bankruptcies throughout the United States;

To coin Money, regulate the Value thereof, and of foreign Coin, and fix the Standard of Weights and Measures;

To provide for the Punishment of counterfeiting the Securities and current Coin of the United States;

To establish Post Offices and post Roads;

To promote the Progress of Science and useful Arts, by securing for limited Times to Authors and Inventors the exclusive Right to their respective Writings and Discoveries;

To constitute Tribunals inferior to the supreme Court;

To define and punish Piracies and Felonies committed on the high Seas, and Offences against the Law of Nations;

To declare War, grant Letters of Marque and Reprisal, and make Rules concerning Captures on Land and Water;

To raise and support Armies, but no Appropriation of Money to that Use shall be for a longer Term than two Years;

To provide and maintain a Navy;

To make Rules for the Government and Regulation of the land and naval Forces;

To provide for calling forth the Militia to execute the Laws of the Union, suppress Insurrections and repel Invasions;

To provide for organizing, arming, and disciplining the Militia, and for governing such Part of them as may be employed in the Service of the United States, reserving to the States respectively, the Appointment of the Officers, and the Authority of training the Militia according to the discipline prescribed by Congress;

To exercise exclusive Legislation in all Cases whatsoever, over such District (not exceeding ten Miles square) as may, by Cession of particular States, and the Acceptance of Congress, become the Seat of the Government of the United States, and to exercise like Authority over all Places purchased by the Consent of the Legislature of the State in which the Same shall be, for the Erection of Forts, Magazines, Arsenals, dock-Yards, and other needful Buildings;—And

To make all Laws which shall be necessary and proper for carrying into Execution the foregoing Powers, and all other Powers vested by this Constitution in the Government of the United States, or in any Department or Officer thereof.

Taxation

Section 8 of the Constitution delegates power to the Congress. One of the basic defects of the Articles of Confederation was the lack of the power "to lay and collect Taxes." The Constitution corrected this.

Congress was granted the power to tax with certain restrictions and limitations. All federal duties, imposts, and excises must be uniform throughout the United States. This means simply that federal tariff duties or internal revenue taxes must be levied uniformly in all parts of the United States. If cigarettes are taxed at $5.00 a thousand in California by the Federal Government, they must be taxed at the same rate in Maine. Section 2 of Article I imposes the provision that "direct taxes" must be apportioned among the states. Direct taxes, for example, are poll taxes and taxes on property imposed because of ownership. When Congress levies a direct tax, it must first decide the exact amount of money desired and then allot to each state the portion of this sum which the state's population bears to the total national population. This is what apportionment means. Direct taxes have only been levied five times in our history. The last time was during the War Between the States. The reason Congress has not employed this method of taxation since the War Between the States is because "apportionment" among the states on the basis of population would result in inequalities because of the differences in the wealth of the various states. When the United States Supreme Court in 1895 held a federal income tax law unconstitutional because it was a direct tax and had not been apportioned, agitation for a constitutional amendment finally resulted in the adoption of the Sixteenth Amendment in 1913. This amendment now permits Congress to "lay and collect taxes on incomes" without apportionment among the several states.

The main sources of federal revenue today are the taxes on our personal income, on the income of business establishments, on the sale and manufacture of certain goods, on money and goods a person inherits, and on imports from foreign nations.

Congress levies taxes to pay the cost of the federal government, to provide for the common defense, and to promote the "General Welfare."

From the time of the Constitutional Convention to within very recent times there has been controversy over what was meant by "general welfare." It has been more or less accepted that the power to lay taxes is for the purpose of paying the debt or providing for the welfare of the nation. On the meaning of "general welfare" James Madison took the position that the grant of power to tax and spend for the welfare of the nation was confined to the powers specified in the Constitution. Hamilton, on the other hand, contended that this clause of the Constitution conferred separate and distinct power from powers enumerated in the Constitution. He held that there was no limit on Congress' taxing power as long as it was *exercised to promote the welfare of the nation.* The United States Supreme Court in 1936 adopted Hamilton's philosophy in the case of United States v. Butler: "The power to tax is not unlimited, its confines are set in the clause which confers it, and not in those of Section 8 which bestow and define the legislative powers of the Congress. It results that the power of Congress to authorize expenditure of public moneys for public purposes is not limited by the direct grants of legislative power found in the Constitution." The court has also held that the Congress could not use the taxing power if it violated the Tenth Amendment. Appropriations for "internal improvements," subsidies, federal grants-in-aid, social security legislation, and unemployment insurance have been held to be constitutional exercises of the taxing and spending power.

Borrowing

The Congress is empowered to raise funds by borrowing money on the credit of the United States. This is a very important power.

The wars we have fought have largely been financed by issuance of government securities. The national debt now amounts to $286,000,000,000. When Congress borrows money, it creates a binding obligation on the American people to pay the debt as stipulated and

UNITED STATES
CUSTOMS

agreed. So important to the solvency, strength, and security of the nation is the public credit that George Washington in his "Farewell Address" called on the American people to cherish the public credit and to use it "as sparingly as possible." Although he was cognizant of the necessity to spend to prevent danger and to be prepared, he urged avoidance of "the accumulation of debt . . . by vigorous exertions in time of peace to discharge the Debts which unavoidable wars may have occasioned, not ungenerously throwing upon posterity the burthen which we ourselves ought to bear."

Commerce

Chaos and confusion resulted under the Articles of Confederation when each state could regulate trade with foreign countries and with every other state (see page 60).

The Constitution gives Congress the power to establish regulations for trade between the United States and foreign nations. These regulations must apply equally to all states. This is an extensive power, for Congress may (1) determine what articles may be imported into the country, (2) state the terms under which importations may take place, (3) ban articles from foreign commerce, and

(4) make tariff regulations. Congress, if it must, can stop foreign trade entirely as it did in the famous "Embargo Acts" in the early history of our country.

During the period of the Napoleonic Wars between England and France, our merchant ships were subjected to onerous regulations of search and seizure. Many of our sailors were seized on the high seas and compelled to serve in the English Navy. Both belligerents flouted our maritime rights. After exhausting all diplomatic channels, Congress, on the recommendation of President Jefferson, passed the Embargo Act of 1807. Under the terms of this act all import and export trade was forbidden. The idea was to keep our merchant marine in our ports. Jefferson thought that our trade was so indispensable that both France and England would relax their rules. It did not work out that way. The rules were not relaxed. Adverse internal economic conditions due to the isolation of America from the rest of the world led to repeal of the Act by Congress in 1809. The Non-Intercourse Act of 1809 was placed on the statute books. It prohibited trade with England and France but permitted trading with the other nations of the world. It also provided that the President by proclamation could restore trade with England and France whenever England revoked its Orders in Council or France rescinded its decrees against American commerce.

But equally as important as the problem of foreign trade was the question of ensuring the flow of goods and services between the various states. Congress was given the right to regulate commerce between the states, thus eliminating any hampering regulations of interstate commerce by the states. This power of Congress has become one of the most far-reaching of all congressional powers, and it is one of the most important limitations placed by the Constitution on the several states. The Supreme Court has given this clause a very broad interpretation over the years so that today "interstate commerce" has come to mean and include operations which come before as well as those which follow "commerce."

What is "commerce"? The Supreme Court has declared that the word "commerce" in the Constitution includes the distribution, purchase, sale, and exchange of goods. Thus, in regard to interstate commerce, a state can be prevented by Congress from giving preference to goods manufactured by its own citizens through the taxation of goods coming from other states.

How does Congress regulate commerce? The development of the applications of this clause has been gradual, and many agencies have been established by Congress in regulating interstate commerce. An examination of a few of these agencies and their functions will give us an understanding of how this clause has been applied.

The Interstate Commerce Commission created in 1887 to regulate the railroads has grown tremendously during the past seventy-two years. It has regulatory supervision over interstate motor carriers, water carriers, pipelines, express companies, and sleeping car companies as well as the rail lines.

The Federal Trade Commission was established to protect the nation from unfair or dishonest practices in interstate commerce. It looks into matters like unfair trade practices, misleading advertising, misrepresentations, and unfair competition.

There are dozens of other agencies which Congress has created to carry out its power to "regulate commerce."

Yet, the states themselves have retained the power to regulate commerce within their own boundaries. Such items of regulation as inspection laws, quarantine and health laws, and laws in regard to bridges, ferries, and highways fall within the jurisdiction of the states. Regulations of this nature are essential to the protection, safety, and welfare of each local area. States cannot pass acts which will be harmful to interstate commerce; on the other hand they can protect and promote the welfare of their citizens.

Naturalization and Bankruptcies

Congress has full power to naturalize foreigners. It passes necessary laws under which foreigners may be made citizens. Congress commenced the enactment of a long line of naturalization statutes in 1790. The power of naturalization belongs solely and wholly to the Congress. No state can impinge upon it, although Congress by statute can allow certain state courts, as well as federal courts, to grant individual naturalization papers. In these instances, the state court is merely acting as an agent of the Federal Government by administering the federal laws.

Congress is also charged with the responsibility of passing uniform laws on the subject of bankruptcies. It is under this clause that federal courts have jurisdiction in bankruptcy cases.

When a person finds that he can no longer pay his debts, he can declare his bankruptcy. A court of law will judge how and to whom his debts are to be paid from whatever money or other assets he has. But the distribution of a debtor's property to his creditors is not the only subject of bankruptcy laws. Under our bankruptcy laws a person in debt is allowed to pay the money he owes without being imprisoned. He can again carry on a business when the people to whom he owes money have received what the courts consider to be a fair payment.

Money

Congress has complete power over money. The states are specifically forbidden to emit bills of credit, coin money, or make anything but gold or silver as legal tender for the payment of debts. The United States has always had two kinds of money: coin and paper. Up to 1933 there usually were gold and silver coins, as well as smaller coins made of the baser metals. Coins are minted by the federal government under direction of the United States Director of the Mint at the two mints at Philadelphia and Denver. Coins in general circulation are the dollar, half dollar, quarter, dime, nickel, and penny. Our paper money is printed only by the Bureau of Engraving and Printing, Treasury Department, Washington, D. C. Denominations of United States paper currency in general circulation today are $1.00, $2.00, $5.00, $10.00, $20.00, $50.00, $100.00, $500.00, $1,000.00, and $5,000.00.

One of the most far-reaching events in American history took place in 1933 when Congress nationalized gold and authorized the return of all gold coins and gold certificates (currency payable in gold) to the United States Treasury for payment in other forms of coin or currency. At the time there were outstanding some $475,000,000 in gold coins and about $600,000,000 in gold certificates. This step was taken because of several reasons. There was hoarding of gold and gold certificates by many of the people, and the new administration was planning to increase the price of gold and to devalue the dollar in order to increase the prices of commodities and, according to President Franklin D. Roosevelt, to cope with the depression. There was, and still is, much controversy over the wisdom of this course of action.

On June 5, 1933, Congress passed a joint resolution declaring it contrary to public policy for anyone to demand payment of an obligation in gold coin or in a particular kind of coin or currency. Thus, Congress abolished the so-called "gold clause" in all obligations both private and public. By other acts of Congress and presidential proclamations, the American dollar was devalued from $25\frac{8}{10}$ grains of gold nine-tenths fine to $15\frac{5}{21}$ grains of gold. In terms of the gold-purchasing power of the American dollar in 1933, it was reduced to a value of 59.06 cents, and the price of gold was increased from $20.67 to $35.00 per ounce.

These drastic changes in our monetary system led to litigation designed to test the validity of Congress' action. By a five to four decision, the Supreme Court decided that the constitutional power of Congress to coin money and regulate the currency of the United States supersedes the provisions of any private contract or obligation which interfered with the exercise of that power, and, therefore, Congress had exercised its constitutional power when it set aside the gold clauses in private contracts. In another five to four decision, the Supreme Court held that Congress could not repudiate its promise to pay its government obligations in gold. However, no one could recover damages unless they could show that Congress' action resulted in damages from breaking its contracts. Since there was no free domestic market for gold in existence, and any gold paid out by the government would have to be surrendered under a government call, it was obviously impossible to prove "damages." Furthermore, Congress immediately passed a law denying the right of anyone after December 31, 1935, to sue the United States Government to recover damages as a result of the abrogation of the gold clauses in government obligations as provided under the joint resolution of June 5, 1933.

Congress has not extensively used its power to fix a standard of weights and measures. It has adopted some standards such as the "wine gallon" as the standard of liquid measurement. The English system of standards has generally been followed as a matter of tradition.

In 1901 Congress created the Bureau of Standards, which was made custodian of standards and which is charged with continually studying and testing existing standards. This bureau engages in extensive research on standards of size, time, quality, and such. In 1918 Congress established standard time zones. States have exercised the power of determining standards in the absence of Congressional legislation. In many states, daylight-savings time is established at certain periods of the year independent of federal legislation.

Punishing Counterfeiters

In order to protect the coins and currency of the United States, Congress has the power to punish counterfeiters. Congress has vested this power in the Treasury Department, which has assigned to its T-men the responsibility of apprehending counterfeiters.

Postal Service

The postal service in the United States has had a long history. As early as 1639 the Colony of Massachusetts designated an official in Boston to take charge of the transmittal of letters. Virginia, in 1657, worked out a system for dispatching official letters from plantation to plantation. In 1672 New York established an intercolonial mail system on a monthly basis between New York City and Boston. Mail delivery in colonial days was uncertain and very slow. In 1710 England took over the colonial mail system and made it part of the British post office. In 1753 Benjamin Franklin became Postmaster General for the colonies, retaining the office until 1774 when the British dismissed him because he supported the colonial cause. However, the Continental Congress made him their Postmaster General until he resigned in 1776 to represent the Congress in France.

On July 17, 1789, Congress authorized the reorganization of the postal service and placed the responsibility of the post offices in the Treasury Department under Alexander Hamilton. It was not until March 9, 1829, that the Postmaster General was made a member of the President's Cabinet.

NEITHER SNOW, NOR RAIN, NOR HEAT, NOR GLOOM OF NIGHT STAYS THESE COURIERS FROM THE SWIFT COMPLETION OF THEIR APPOINTED ROUNDS

Under its power to establish post offices and post roads, Congress has created thousands of post offices and an extensive system of mail distribution by ships, railroads, and planes. Parcel post, postal money orders, and postal savings are extensions of this power. The Congress also exercises national police power to protect the public against abuses and evils as a result of the use of the United States mails. For example, there are stringent national laws against defrauding the public or corrupting its morals through the mails. Congress appears to be able to do anything which it considers necessary to insure the safe, speedy, and prompt delivery of the mails.

Patents and Copyrights

Congress is given the power to provide for the issuance of patents and copyrights in order to provide for the promotion of science and the useful arts. Patents are granted by the Patent Office of the Department of Commerce. Patents are granted for a period of seventeen years and are generally not renewable. It also registers trade-marks. Copyrights are administered by the Librarian of Congress. A copyright is granted for a period of twenty-eight years and may be renewed only once.

Lower Courts

The power of Congress to create tribunals inferior to the Supreme Court will be discussed under the judiciary provisions of the Constitution. (See pages 145-147.)

Punishing Piracy

Congress defines and punishes piracies and felonies committed on the high seas and offenses against the law of nations.

When the Constitution of the United States was adopted, piracy on the high seas was quite common. For example, small nations located on the Mediterranean Sea in North Africa practiced piracy and plundered ships plying in the Mediterranean Sea unless a tribute was paid to the rulers of these nations.

For a number of years our own country annually paid a sum of money to these pirates in order to maintain peace. During Jefferson's administration the pirates demanded an increase in these payments. President Jefferson decided that the time had come when we should fight rather than pay tribute; therefore, in 1801 he dispatched the Navy to fight the pirates that were operating off Tripoli. The most famous exploit of the war was Stephen Decatur's burning of the captured frigate *Philadelphia* in Tripoli harbor without the loss of an American life. This war with Tripoli ended in 1804, and from that moment on the United States never again paid tribute to anyone. Our ships sailed the seas in safety.

Under international law, all vessels on the seas and oceans must be registered to a nation and must fly that nation's flag as a means of identification.

Crimes committed on the high seas on board an American vessel are subject to the courts of the United States. Whenever our vessels are in foreign waters, the jurisdiction of the United States is gener-

Stephen Decatur and the Burning of the *Philadelphia* in Tripoli Harbor

ally exclusive except in certain cases. Chief Justice Waite of the United States Supreme Court in 1886 in the Wildenhaus Case said: "Disorders which disturb only the peace of the ship, or those on board, are to be dealt with exclusively by the sovereignty of the home of the ship; but those which disturb the public peace may be suppressed, and if need be, the offenders punished by the proper authorities of the local jurisdiction."

Declaring War and the Armed Forces

Congress has the following war powers: 1. declare war; 2. grant letters of marque and reprisals; 3. make rules concerning captures on land and water; 4. raise and support armies; 5. make rules for the government and regulation of the land and naval forces; 6. call out the militia to execute the laws, suppress insurrections, and repel invasions; and 7. provide for organizing, arming, and disciplining the militia.

Under the Articles of Confederation it took the consent of nine states for the Congress of the Confederation to declare war. This necessity of concurrence of the states was a weakness which the fathers of our Constitution readily corrected by unquestionably vesting the power to declare war in the Congress of the United States. All power involving war and dealing with it is vested with the Federal Government and not with the states. As is readily evident, the war powers conferred by the Constitution are tremendous. The President, as commander in chief, may use the armed forces at his disposal to protect our interests and thereby create "a state of war," or by his policy of diplomacy he may make war inevitable. However, only Congress can declare war. This it generally does by adoption of a joint resolution of both Houses of Congress. It can declare a war terminated by the same procedure.

During World War II there was very extensive legislation passed by Congress under its war power. The Priorities Act of 1941 gave the President of the United States power to allocate any material necessary to facilitate the defense of our country. By the second War Powers Act of 1942 the authority of the President was extended to facilities. It was under these acts that consumer rationing was administered by the Office of Price Administration and that the control of materials and production was undertaken by the War Production Board. The War Labor Disputes Act permitted the President to take over plants when they were closed by strikes. These and many other acts during the war brought the entire population within the scope of mobilization. The Constitution places emphasis upon supporting armies, as well as raising them. Thus Congress has the power to mobilize the industrial establishments of the nation in time of war as well as the power to resort to conscription. The military machine and the civilian establishment to support it during World War II was unparalleled in American history. The next war will probably bring total mobilization of every resource of the nation.

Congress has established academies for the training of officer personnel. There is the United States Military Academy at West Point, New York; the United States Naval Academy at Annapolis, Maryland; the United States Air Force Academy at Colorado Springs, Colorado; the United States Coast Guard Academy at New London, Connecticut; and the United States Merchant Marine Academy at Kings Point, New York.

It is extremely fortunate that the fathers of our Constitution provided for the civilian control of the armed forces of the United States. Congress must appropriate the money for the maintenance of the military and naval establishments, and it can only do it for a period of two years. The commander in chief is a civilian: the President of the United States. The Secretary of Defense is required by an act of Congress to be a civilian. Congress must pass the basic legislation for the mobilization of the nation. The drafters of our Constitution wanted to prevent the establishment of any military dictatorship.

Raising the Flag at Iwo Jima

Federal Lands

Congress governs the District of Columbia by acting as the legislative body of the District and by providing for appointment of three commissioners by the President. The commissioners are administrative officers with ministerial powers given them by congressional statutes. The District was established by Acts of Congress on July 16, 1790, and March 3, 1791. The United States took jurisdiction of the District in December of 1800. It was President Adams who transferred the seat of government from Philadelphia to Washington.

Wherever the nation establishes forts, magazines, arsenals, post offices, dockyards, and such, the nation controls the land to the exclusion of the states.

Elastic Clause

Congress may make all laws "necessary and proper" to carry into execution the powers which the Constitution has delegated to the government of the United States or any of its departments or officers. This is the famous "implied power" clause of the Constitution, which is also called the "elastic clause." Under this power not only can Congress pass all statutes necessary to carry out the powers which are delegated to it by the Constitution but it can and does have the authority to pass statutes that may be necessary to carry out all powers "implied" from the delegated power. It is under this clause that many of the unforeseen conditions of our daily life are coped with. Under the theory that it was necessary and proper to the commerce clause, Congress passed laws regulating steamboat companies and the railroads, telegraph and telephone companies, radio and television broadcasting, and the airlines. None of these developments were foreseen when the Constitution was drafted. The generation of power by the federal government through the Tennessee Valley Authority was held to be a constitutional exercise of power "implied" under the commerce clause and the war powers. "Implied" power is not unlimited power. Congress can only exercise "implied" power provided it is tied to a "delegated" power. As Chief Justice Marshall said in McCulloch v. Maryland: "Let the end be legitimate, let it be within the scope of the Constitution, and all means which are appropriate, which are plainly adopted to that end, which are not prohibited, but consistent with the letter and spirit of the Constitution, are constitutional."

The great expansion in federal authority which has taken place since the adoption of the Constitution has come about through the "implied" powers clause of our Constitution.

Limitations of Congress' Power

SECTION 9

The Migration or Importation of such Persons as any of the States now existing shall think proper to admit, shall not be prohibited by the Congress prior to the Year one thousand eight hundred and eight, but a Tax or duty may be imposed on such Importation, not exceeding ten dollars for each Person.

The Privilege of the Writ of Habeas Corpus shall not be suspended, unless when in Cases of Rebellion or Invasion the public Safety may require it.

No Bill of Attainder or ex post facto Law shall be passed.

No Capitation, or other direct, Tax shall be laid, unless in Proportion to the Census or Enumeration herein before directed to be taken.

No Tax or Duty shall be laid on Articles exported from any State.

No Preference shall be given by any Regulation of Commerce or Revenue to the Ports of one State over those of another: nor shall Vessels bound to, or from, one State, be obliged to enter, clear, or pay Duties in another.

No Money shall be drawn from the Treasury, but in Consequence of Appropriations made by Law; and a regular Statement and Account of the Receipts and Expenditures of all public Money shall be published from time to time.

No Title of Nobility shall be granted by the United States: And no Person holding any Office of Profit or Trust under them, shall, without the Consent of the Congress, accept of any present, Emolument, Office, or Title, of any kind whatever, from any King, Prince, or foreign State.

The purpose of Section 9 of Article I is to place restraints upon the power of Congress and the national government. It is important to know that in no way does this section apply to the states in their regulation of domestic affairs. There are ten things which Congress cannot do under this section:

1. Congress was forbidden to prohibit the importation of slaves prior to 1808. In 1807 Congress passed an act ending the slave trade.

2. Congress cannot suspend the writ of *habeas corpus* except in cases of rebellion or invasion. *Habeas corpus* is a legal writ requiring a person to be brought before a judge or court for an investigation of why the person is imprisoned. Any person imprisoned without just cause can thus win his liberation with the help of a writ of *habeas corpus*. This is one of the most important of all our personal liberties. It is the greatest of the safeguards of personal liberty embodied in the common law. This is the only place in the Constitution where the writ of *habeas corpus* is mentioned.

3. and 4. Congress is prohibited from passing a *bill of attainder* or an *ex post facto law*. A *bill of attainder* is a legislative act which punishes a person without a trial and "taints the blood" so such a person cannot inherit property and his children cannot inherit from him. There are many instances in English history and several in American colonial history which made this provision in the Constitution a wise one. Any law, which makes criminal an act which was not criminal when committed, or which inflicts a greater punishment than when the crime was committed, is an *ex post facto* law and is forbidden by our Constitution.

5. Congress cannot lay any direct tax unless it is in proportion to the census. (See discussion on taxing power of Congress, pages 112-113).

6. Congress is forbidden from levying a tax or duty on articles exported from any state.

7. Congress cannot by a regulation of commerce or revenue give preferences to the ports of one state over those of another state.

8. Congress cannot levy duties or tonnage taxes on vessels bound from one state to another.

9. No money can be drawn from the United States Treasury except through an appropriation made by law. This clause limits the power of the President and other officers of the United States in that Congress must appropriate the money to be spent.

10. No title of nobility can be granted by the United States, and no person holding an office under the United States can accept any present, office, or title from a king, prince, or foreign

state except with the consent of Congress. Our forefathers were concerned over the possibility of foreign influences upon our government, and they felt that this provision was necessary for the protection of the nation. Congress from time to time makes exceptions, such as permitting members of the armed forces to receive foreign decorations.

Limitations on the States

SECTION 10

No State shall enter into any Treaty, Alliance, or Confederation; grant Letters of Marque and Reprisal; coin Money; emit Bills of Credit; make any Thing but gold and silver Coin a Tender in Payment of Debts; pass any Bill of Attainder, ex post facto Law, or Law impairing the Obligation of Contracts, or grant any Title of Nobility.

No State shall without the Consent of the Congress, lay any Imposts or Duties on Imports or Exports, except what may be absolutely necessary for executing its inspection Laws: and the net Produce of all Duties and Imposts, laid by any State on Imports or Exports, shall be for the Use of the Treasury of the United States; and all such Laws shall be subject to the Revision and Control of the Congress.

No State shall, without the Consent of Congress, lay any Duty of Tonnage, keep Troops, or Ships of War in time of Peace, enter into any Agreement or Compact with another State, or with a foreign Power, or engage in War, unless actually invaded, or in such imminent Danger as will not admit of delay.

Section 10 imposes limitations upon the several states in order to prevent encroachments on the powers of the national government. In general, this Section also imposes the same prohibitions on the states that Section 9 places on the Federal government. The states are forbidden to pass bills of attainder, ex post facto laws, laws impairing the obligations of a contract, or to grant titles of nobility. Furthermore, no state is permitted to enter into any treaty or alliance, grant letters of marque, coin money, issue paper money, or make it a legal tender.

No state can hamper trade by taxing the exports or imports of another state. The imports and exports spoken of here refer to articles imported from or exported to foreign countries and passing through other states to their destination. This clause does not prohibit a state from taxing goods originating in and brought from other states; such taxes by states are forbidden as an invasion of the right of Congress to regulate interstate commerce (see page 115).

Yet a state can inspect goods coming from a foreign nation and charge a nominal fee to cover inspection costs. If a state were to tax imports above a charge for inspection, Congress would have to approve, and the tax would go to the federal treasury. Thus, there would not be much advantage to a state taxing such imports.

No state may keep troops or ships of war or enter into any agreement with any other state or with a foreign power, without the consent of Congress. A state cannot engage in war unless actually invaded. These restraints were considered necessary to the successful operation of the Federal Government.

Article II THE EXECUTIVE

The President

SECTION 1

The executive Power shall be vested in a President of the United States of America. He shall hold his Office during the Term of four Years, and, together with the Vice President, chosen for the same Term, be elected, as follows:

Each State shall appoint, in such Manner as the Legislature thereof may direct, a Number of Electors, equal to the whole Number of Senators and Representatives to which the State may be entitled in the Congress; but no Senator or Representative, or Person holding an Office of Trust or Profit under the United States, shall be appointed an Elector.

The Electors shall meet in their respective States, and vote by Ballot for two Persons, of whom one at least shall not be an Inhabitant of the same State with themselves. And they shall make a List of all the Persons voted for, and of the Number of Votes for each; which List they shall sign and certify, and transmit sealed to the Seat of the Government of the United States, directed to the President of the Senate. The President of the Senate shall, in the Presence of the Senate and House of Representatives, open all the Certificates, and the Votes shall then be counted. The Person having

the greatest Number of Votes shall be the President, if such Number
be a Majority of the whole Number of Electors appointed; and if
there be more than one who have such Majority, and have an equal
Number of Votes, then the House of Representatives shall immedi-
ately chuse by Ballot one of them for President; and if no Person
have a Majority, then from the five highest on the List the said
House shall in like Manner chuse the President. But in chusing the
President, the Votes shall be taken by States, the Representation
from each State having one Vote; A quorum for this Purpose shall
consist of a Member or Members from two thirds of the States, and
a Majority of all the States shall be necessary to a Choice. In every
Case, after the Choice of the President, the Person having the greatest
Number of Votes of the Electors shall be Vice President. But if
there should remain two or more who have equal Votes, the Senate
shall chuse from them by Ballot the Vice President.

The Congress may determine the Time of chusing the Electors,
and the Day on which they shall give their Votes; which Day shall be
the same throughout the United States.

No Person except a natural born Citizen, *or a Citizen of the United*
States, at the time of the Adoption of this Constitution shall be
eligible to the Office of President; neither shall any Person be eligible
to that Office who shall not have attained to the Age of thirty-five
Years, and been fourteen Years a Resident within the United States.

In Case of the Removal of the President from Office, or of his
Death, Resignation, or Inability to discharge the Powers and Duties
of the said Office, the Same shall devolve on the Vice President, and
the Congress may by Law provide for the Case of Removal, Death,
Resignation or Inability, both of the President and Vice President,
declaring what Officer shall then act as President, and such Officer
shall act accordingly, until the Disability be removed, or a President
shall be elected.

The President shall, at stated Times, receive for his Services, a
Compensation, which shall neither be encreased nor diminished during the Period for which he shall have been elected, and he shall not
receive within that Period any other Emolument from the United
States, or any of them.

Before he enter on the Execution of his Office, he shall take the
following Oath or Affirmation:—"I do solemnly swear (or affirm) that
I will faithfully execute the Office of President of the United States,
and will to the best of my Ability, preserve, protect and defend the
Constitution of the United States."

Oath of Office of the President. *I do solemnly swear (or affirm) that I will faithfully execute the Office of President of the United States, and will, to the best of my Ability, preserve, protect, and defend the Constitution of the United States.*

Under the Constitution the executive power is placed in the hands of the President of the United States. There was considerable discussion during the Constitutional Convention about the function of the executive. Discussion on this department of government showed that the Convention changed its mind frequently during its deliberation of what the nature of the executive was to be. A suggestion for a plural executive, one to represent the small states and one to represent the large, was made. Another proposal suggested that there be three executives: one each to represent New England, the Middle States, and the South, thus giving each region a president, or part of the executive. On June 1, 1787, Wilson of Pennsylvania moved that the executive powers be vested in one person, but his motion did not carry on that day. Randolph of Virginia made a motion that the executive consist of three persons, but it also failed to carry. Many members of the Convention advocated an executive council because they felt that no one man should be entrusted with the various powers and duties that an executive should have. However, final decision of the Convention showed that this belief was in the minority.

Further deliberation loomed regarding tenure. The question of number of years that the President should serve brought forth suggestions running from a two-year term to life. As the discussion on this question proceeded, the Convention came more and more to the belief that the term of office should be long enough to give stability to the office. It voted, at one time, to give the President of the United States a seven-year term but to make him ineligible for re-election. On September 4, 1787, two weeks prior to the adjournment of the Convention, it was voted that the term of the President be for four years with no limitations on eligibility for re-election. This provision remained unchanged until the Twenty-second Amendment was ratified in 1951.

The Seal of the United States

The President and Vice President are elected by presidential electors. Each state has as many presidential electors as it has Senators and Representatives in Congress. (There are currently 537 presidential electors, and 269 electoral votes are needed to elect. The number of electors will revert to 535 in 1960 unless Congress should pass a law increasing the number of Representatives [see page 102.])

The method of electing the President and Vice President was also debated at length in the Constitutional Convention, and several different plans were proposed. These were the election by the states, each state having one vote; by electors chosen by the state legislatures or the people; by the state legislatures; by the Senate; by the Congress in joint session; by the House of Representatives;

by direct vote of the people; by the governors of the states; by the governors of the states with an advisory council; by twenty-five electors apportioned according to the total number of states; nomination of the candidates by the House of Representatives and election by the Senate.

On July 17, 1787, it was agreed that the Congress should elect the President. On July 19 it was moved to reconsider. After debate and reconsideration, it was voted to elect by presidential electors. Five days later, on July 24, it was agreed again to allow Congress to elect the President of the United States, but on September 6, by a vote of nine states to two, the electoral college system was adopted. Originally suggested by Hamilton, this system entitled each state to as many electors as it had Senators and Representatives in Congress.

The Electoral College

It was the concept of the framers of our form of government that each elector would, meeting with his colleagues in each state, thoughtfully and carefully determine who was to be President and Vice President and cast their electoral ballots accordingly. The practice of American politics did not work out that way. Instead a system grew up outside the Constitution which brought into being the national parties. Each party's candidate for President and Vice President is placed into running every four years by national nominating conventions. Delegates to the national convention are chosen in various ways. Some states name their delegates through their state party conventions or state central committees. In others there is a presidential primary election in which the party members directly name the delegates.

The presidential electors are pledged to vote for the party's candidates. Some Southern states, however, have passed laws which enables the electors to vote for candidates other than the nominees of their party.

As a result of the party system, politics has come to play a highly important role in the election of the President and in the relationship between Congress and the Executive.

The Constitution provided that the electors vote for two individuals and that the individual receiving the largest majority of the electoral college should be declared President and the man with the second largest majority should be declared Vice President. In other words, no provision was made for designating which of the two votes of each elector was for President and which for Vice President. (This was corrected by the adoption of the Twelfth Amendment in 1804.) In the absence of a majority vote for any candidate by the electoral college, the election of the President is the responsibility of the House of Representatives, and that of the Vice President the responsibility of the Senate. When electing a President or Vice President, each state in Congress casts one vote. A majority of the States is necessary for election.

Only twice in American history has the electoral college failed to elect the President. The first time was in the election of 1800, when the party system had already fastened itself upon the country. The Democrat-Republicans, then a single party, cast their electoral votes for Jefferson and Burr without distinguishing between Jefferson, the presidential candidate, and Burr, the vice-presidential candidate. A tie in the presidency resulted, and it became the duty of the House of Representatives to elect the President of the United States. The House elected Jefferson as President, and Burr became Vice President.

As a result of this election, the Twelfth Amendment was adopted in 1804 providing that henceforth the electoral college should designate for whom it was voting for President and Vice President.

The second time the House of Representatives chose the President was in the election of 1824, in which no presidential candidate received a majority of the electoral vote. In the session of 1825 the House of Representatives chose John Quincy Adams as President.

Only once in the history of the country has the United States Senate chosen the Vice President. In the election of 1836 the Democrats failed to concentrate on one candidate for Vice President of the United States, no candidate received a majority, and in the senatorial session of February, 1837, the Senate elected Richard M. Johnson, Democrat of Kentucky, as Vice President.

To be President or Vice President of the United States, a person must be a natural-born citizen, thirty-five years of age, and fourteen years a resident within the United States.

Presidential Succession

Whenever the President dies, resigns, or is unable to discharge his powers and duties, he is succeeded by the Vice President. Congress has the power to provide by law for the presidential succession in case there is no Vice President. On July 18, 1947, Con-

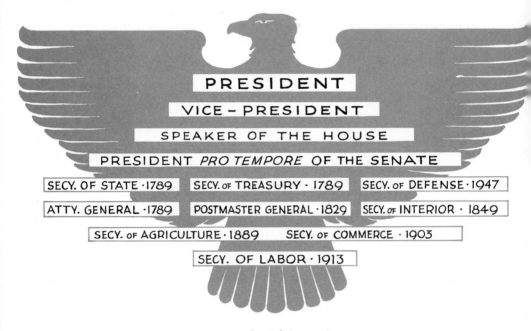

PRESIDENT

VICE - PRESIDENT

SPEAKER OF THE HOUSE

PRESIDENT *PRO TEMPORE* OF THE SENATE

| SECY. OF STATE ·1789 | SECY. OF TREASURY · 1789 | SECY. OF DEFENSE·1947 |
| ATTY. GENERAL ·1789 | POSTMASTER GENERAL · 1829 | SECY. OF INTERIOR · 1849 |

SECY. OF AGRICULTURE · 1889   SECY. OF COMMERCE · 1903

SECY. OF LABOR · 1913

Presidential Succession

gress passed a Presidential Succession Act. It provided that after the Vice President, the Speaker of the House shall become President. In case of his disqualification or inability to serve, the President pro tempore of the Senate becomes President, then the members of the Cabinet become eligible in the order in which their offices were created. Both the Speaker and the President pro tempore would have to resign as members of the Senate or House. Any Cabinet member becoming President would have to resign his Cabinet post. Seven Vice Presidents have succeeded to the presidency upon the death of the President: John Tyler, Millard Fillmore, Andrew Johnson, Chester Arthur, Theodore Roosevelt, Calvin Coolidge, and Harry Truman.

On September 24, 1955, President Eisenhower suffered a coronary thrombosis. This set off a discussion as to whether the President was capable of carrying out his duties and resulted in congressional debate over the legal problems and constitutional questions involved. Congress has never defined "inability to discharge the Powers and Duties of the said Office. . . ." In 1881, President

Dwight D. Eisenhower

Garfield was ill for 80 days preceding his death. Between September, 1919, and March, 1921, President Wilson was unable much of the time to carry out his duties. The powers and duties of the presidency in both these instances were not transferred to the Vice President for fear that should the President recover, there might be a question as to regaining the office.

For three years now we have been debating such questions as: How should presidential disability be defined and who should determine when the President is incapacitated? On March 3, 1958, President Eisenhower announced that he and Vice President Nixon had come. to an understanding as to what action to take if the President became disabled. There were three points to the agreement as reported by the *Congressional Quarterly.*

1. "In the event of inability the President would . . . if possible . . . so inform the Vice President, and the Vice President would serve as Acting President, exercising the powers and duties of the Office until the inability had ended.
2. In the event of an inability which would prevent the President from so communicating with the Vice President, the Vice President, after such consultation as seems to him appropriate under the circumstances, would decide upon the devolution of the powers and duties of the Office and would serve as Acting President until the inability had ended.
3. The President, in either event, would determine when the inability had ended and at that time would resume the full exercise of the powers and duties of the Office."

Speaker Rayburn criticized this arrangement with the comment: "I don't know how they are going to create an office of Acting President. I don't see how you can have someone carrying on the duties of President without taking an oath." Attorney General Rogers replied that no oath was necessary and furthermore that he was confident the courts would uphold his point of view.

Following the public announcement of this agreement, action was proposed by several Senators and Representatives. However, Congress adjourned without enactment of any legislation or the passage of a constitutional amendment.

In the Senate there seemed to be some bipartisan sentiment for a proposed constitutional amendment which provided that if the President declared his disability in writing, the Vice President would become Acting President. If the President were unable to declare his own disability, a majority of the heads of the Executive Departments would declare it. The President could declare himself recovered and assume his presidential powers on seven days' notice. Should there be a dispute, the Vice President and a majority of the Cabinet could ask Congress to resolve the question. Unless two-thirds of each House agreed that the President was still incapacitated, the President would resume his post. Congress adjourned without taking action on this or the other proposals that have been introduced on this subject.

The President receives compensation of $100,000 per annum (taxable) and an allowance of $50,000 annually (taxable) as an expense fund and $40,000 (nontaxable) for travel and entertainment. Former Presidents receive a lifetime pension of $25,000 per annum. Widows of former Presidents receive $10,000 per annum.

Presidential Powers

SECTION 2

The President shall be Commander in Chief of the Army and Navy of the United States, and of the Militia of the several States, when called into the actual Service of the United States; he may require the Opinion, in writing, of the principal Officer in each of the executive Departments, upon any Subject relating to the Duties of their respective Offices, and he shall have Power to grant Reprieves and Pardons for Offences against the United States, except in Cases of Impeachment.

He shall have Power, by and with the Advice and Consent of the Senate, to make Treaties, provided two thirds of the Senators present concur; and he shall nominate, and by and with the Advice and Consent of the Senate, shall appoint Ambassadors, other public Ministers and Consuls, Judges of the supreme Court, and all other Officers of the United States, whose Appointments are not herein otherwise provided for, and which shall be established by Law; but the Congress may by Law vest the Appointment of such inferior Officers, as they think proper, in the President alone, in the Courts of Law, or in the Heads of Departments.

The President shall have Power to fill up all Vacancies that may happen during the Recess of the Senate, by granting Commissions which shall expire at the End of their next Session.

The office of President of the United States is one of the most powerful and important in the world. The powers which the Constitution confers upon him are extensive and far-reaching in their consequences. Read Section 2 above very carefully. Note that he

Herbert Hoover

is the commander in chief of the Army and Navy of the United States and of the militia when it is in the service of the United States. He makes rules and regulations for the government of the armed forces, which have the full force of law. Without waiting for action by Congress, he can use the armed forces to put down an insurrection or to repel an invasion. Lincoln, in 1861, ordered the provisioning of Fort Sumter, and the consequence was the War Between the States.

The President's war powers are enormous. He may invade enemy territory and set up a military government. He may declare a blockade of foreign ports and employ secret agents to get information about the enemy. President Franklin D. Roosevelt brought many war agencies into existence by executive order under his war powers. Under the Constitution, the President could, if he wished, actually take command in the field. This has never happened, but Lincoln did issue orders for a general advance of the Army of the Potomac in 1862. In 1918, President Wilson settled the question of the independent American command on the Western Front. It was President Truman who in 1945 ordered the dropping of the atomic bomb on Nagasaki and Hiroshima. The President can requisition property and compel services from citizens of the U. S.

Yet the President as the commander in chief is dependent on Congress for approval of the budget of the armed forces, and the fact that the President, a civilian, is the commander in chief works to prevent a military officer from taking away the Federal Government's powers and establishing a dictatorship.

Nowhere in the Constitution is there any mention of the Cabinet. In Article II, Section 2, Clause 1, of the Constitution there is

138

reference to the fact that the President may require the opinion in writing of "the principal Officer in each of the executive Departments." This is the only indirect reference to "Cabinet." There is nothing which requires the President to consult his Cabinet or to abide by its advice. Cabinet meetings can be dispensed with by the President at any time.

The President may grant pardons and reprieves except in cases of impeachment. The President's pardoning power extends only to offenses

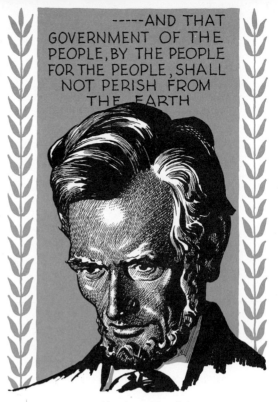

-----AND THAT GOVERNMENT OF THE PEOPLE, BY THE PEOPLE FOR THE PEOPLE, SHALL NOT PERISH FROM THE EARTH

Abraham Lincoln

against the United States. He may pardon a person or grant amnesty to groups of persons. Amnesty is defined as a general pardoning of offenses against the government. President Johnson, in 1865, 1867, and 1868, granted amnesty to the Confederates, and President Theodore Roosevelt, in 1902, granted amnesty to the followers of Aquinaldo in the Philippines.

Originally, the Constitutional Convention gave to the Senate the power to make treaties, and also to appoint ambassadors and judges of the Supreme Court. On September 7, 1787, after long debate, this was changed to provide the provision now in our Constitution. The President alone negotiates a treaty. However, once the President submits the treaty to the Senate, the Senate may ratify, reject, or accept it with amendments or with reservations. If the President does not like the amendments or reservations, he may abandon the treaty.

Since World War II there has been considerable discussion about "executive agreements" which have the full force of a treaty and which may supersede a law of Congress or the law of a state.

139

Theodore Roosevelt

International agreements can be entered into without approval of the Senate. This power, it is contended, flows from the President's position as head of foreign relations and from his power as commander in chief. An "executive agreement" is an understanding between our President and the head of one or more other nations wherein each agrees to a given course of action. It is only binding as long as the President is in office. It has the same force in law as a treaty, but ratification by the senate is not required.

Congress has, from time to time, authorized executive agreements within the field of its powers such as postal agreements, trade-mark, copyright, and reciprocal trade agreements. There are many instances of executive agreements prior to World War II. In 1817 President Monroe, by executive agreement, brought about elimination of armaments on the Great Lakes. In 1882, and again in 1896, we entered into an agreement with Mexico giving each country the right to pursue Indian raiders across the international border. In 1900 President McKinley, relying on the fact that he was commander in chief, consummated an executive agreement under which we contributed 5,000 men and a naval force to rescue the legations in Peking. He also accepted the Boxer Indemnity Protocol without reference to the Senate. In 1908 Theodore Roosevelt gave sanction to the Root-Takahira Agreement to uphold the *status quo* in the Pacific and maintain the principle of equal opportunity for commerce and industry in China. In 1917

140

1932 1936 1940 1944

Franklin Delano Roosevelt

Woodrow Wilson ordered the negotiation of the Lansing-Ishii Agreement under which the United States recognized Japan's "special interests" in China, and Japan agreed to the principle of the open door in China.

However, the executive agreement as an instrument of foreign policy reached its apex under President Franklin D. Roosevelt. On November 16, 1933, through a series of notes sent from President Roosevelt to Maxim M. Litvinov, the People's Commissar in Foreign Affairs, the United States recognized Russia in return for certain pledges. In June of 1940 President Roosevelt entered into two executive agreements, one with Canada and one with Great Britain. The Canadian agreement provided that a Permanent Joint Board on Defense be set up to consider the defense of the northern half of the Western Hemisphere. The Hull-Lothian Agreement of September 2, 1940, provided for lease to the United States of a number of British bases in the British West Atlantic in return for fifty overaged destroyers. We also entered into an agreement with the Danish Minister to the United States for the American occupation of Greenland for the duration of the war for purposes of defense. There were other even more famous agreements after the United States became involved in World War II: Cairo, Teheran, Malta, and Potsdam, for example. The loans and gifts of forty billions of dollars' worth of munitions and other aid to our allies during the war were negotiated under the

141

Harry S. Truman

terms of the Lend-Lease Act of March 11, 1941, wherein Congress authorized the President to enter into executive agreements for this purpose. These, and the executive agreements growing out of our participation in the United Nations, led to the introduction of constitutional amendments seeking to curb and control executive agreements, but the proponents were unable to muster sufficient strength to pass the amendment.

The President, with the approval of the Senate, appoints ambassadors, consuls, ministers, judges, and other officers of the United States. As the federal administration has grown in size, the President has been given the task of appointing a growing list of important officials, such as the head of the Atomic Energy Commission and the Federal Communication Commission. Yet, the Senate exercises its right of passing on these appointments, using its power of acting as a check on the President. We have already seen how the colonial governor's council had the power to approve or reject the appointment of officials to the governor's administration (see page 25), a right given to the Senate in the Constitution.

The Senate seldom rejects a presidential nomination. In all of American history there have only been eight instances of a rejection of a nomination to a Cabinet post. In 1925 the Senate rejected President Coolidge's nomination of Charles Warren as Attorney General. Recently, 1959, President Eisenhower's nomination of Lewis Strauss as Secretary of Commerce failed of confirmation by three votes. Presidents sometimes withdraw their nominees if it appears that the Senate is apt to reject them. In some instances, the nominee himself requests that the President withdraw his name. During the Truman administration, Ed Pauley of California withdrew his name after the President had nominated him as Under Secretary of the Navy.

Several million federal positions are now under civil service. In 1883 Congress passed the Civil Service Act and created the Civil Service Commission. This act gave the President the power to determine who was to be under civil service (classified service) and who was not (unclassified). Though the act has been amended many times since 1883, the President is still the person responsible for the determination of what agencies of the Federal Government operate under "classified" or "unclassified" service. On the other hand, Congress has the power to change this by appropriate legislation. When the Pendleton Act of 1883 went into operation, there were 14,000 federal employees placed under civil service (these were primarily in the Treasury and in the Post Office Department). Today there are only about 175,000 federal jobs out of two and three-quarter million which are *not* under civil service.

The President and Congress

SECTION 3

He shall from time to time give to the Congress Information of the State of the Union, and recommend to their Consideration such Measures as he shall judge necessary and expedient; he may, on extraordinary Occasions, convene both Houses, or either of them, and in Case of Disagreement between them, with Respect to the Time of Adjournment, he may adjourn them to such Time as he shall think proper; he shall receive Ambassadors and other public Ministers; he shall take Care that the Laws be faithfully executed, and shall Commission all the Officers of the United States.

Through his duty to give the Congress information on the state of the union, the President exercises legislative leadership, and, as head of the political party which elects him, he may greatly influence legislation itself. There is no subject today upon which the President cannot communicate with Congress.

Woodrow Wilson

The FOURTEEN POINTS

Presidents Washington and Adams followed the practice of appearing before Congress to deliver their "messages," but President Jefferson set the precedent of transmitting the message in writing. President Wilson restored the practice of appearing in person to deliver the President's annual message.

The President is charged by the Constitution to "take care that the laws be faithfully executed." This, in effect, makes him the chief law enforcement officer of the United States. Many agencies of the Federal Government and their personnel, including the armed forces, are available to the President in carrying out this broad and far-reaching presidential power.

Although the President has on numerous occasions called Congress into "extra" or "special" sessions, he has never exercised his power to adjourn the Houses of Congress.

Impeachment

SECTION 4

The President, Vice President and all civil Officers of the United States, shall be removed from Office on Impeachment for, and Conviction of, Treason, Bribery, or other high Crimes and Misdemeanors.

The President, the Vice President, and all civil officers of the United States can be removed by impeachment proceedings, but not members of Congress. Only once was a President impeached. In 1867 President Johnson was impeached by the House of Representatives, but the Senate found him not guilty of the impeachment charges. In all of American history there have only been four instances of conviction of impeachment. All were judges of federal courts.

An official can be impeached for treason, which is defined in the Constitution as levying war against the United States or giving aid to her enemies (Article III, Section 3, Clause 1).

Bribery is trying to influence a judge or public official by means of gifts or favors. "Other high Crimes or Misdemeanors" refers to offenses of a serious nature.

The only punishment which can be given a public official found guilty is that he be removed from his public office; he would be denied his right to a trial by jury if he was given any other punishment. Yet he can be tried by a civil court with a jury for his crimes.

Article III JUDICIARY

The Supreme Court

SECTION 1

The judicial Power of the United States shall be vested in one supreme Court, and in such inferior Courts as the Congress may from time to time ordain and establish. The judges, both of the supreme and inferior Courts, shall hold their Offices during good Behaviour, and shall, at stated Times, receive for their Services, a Compensation, which shall not be diminished during their Continuance in Office.

This article places the judicial power of the United States in the Supreme Court and in such inferior courts as Congress "may from time to time ordain and establish." All federal judges are appointed by the President with the advice and consent of the Senate. They hold their offices during "good Behaviour," so they can only be removed by impeachment. The great importance of the courts in our form of government was well set forth by Justice Story when he said: "Where there is no judicial department to interpret, pronounce, and execute the law, to decide controversies, and to enforce rights, the government must either perish by its own imbecility, or the other departments of government must usurp powers, for the purpose of commanding oebdience, to the destruction of liberty. The will of those who govern will become, under such circumstances, absolute and despotic; it is wholly immaterial, whether power is vested in a single tyrant or in an assembly of tyrants."

The Constitution provides for one Supreme Court but makes no reference as to its size or its composition. Congress determines these matters. The first Supreme Court established in 1789 consisted of a Chief Justice and five Associate Justices. The number of judges was decreased to five in 1801 and restored to six in 1802. In 1837 the Supreme Court was fixed at nine judges. In 1863 the number was increased to ten and reduced in 1866 to seven. In 1869 the Congress fixed the number of judges at nine. For ninety years there has been no change in the number of judges on the court. The Chief Justice receives a salary of $35,500 per annum; and the Associate Justices, $35,000. When Supreme Court justices reach seventy years of age and have ten years of service, they can, if they wish, retire at full salary. They can retire at full salary at sixty-five if they have fifteen years of service.

The Constitution also gave Congress the power to create all the courts inferior to the Supreme Court.

Congress created the United States District Courts, which have jurisdiction over most cases involving crimes against the United States and civil cases involving the laws of the United States. Between the District Courts and the Supreme Court lie the United States Courts of Appeals. These serve as courts of appeal from the United States District Courts, from the special courts created by Congress, and from certain federal boards and commissions such as the Federal Power Commission and the Interstate Commerce Commission. The judges of these courts hold their offices during good behavior. The District Judges receive a salary of $22,500 per annum. The judges of the Courts of Appeals receive $25,500.

Congress created the United States Court of Claims. It hears all cases which involve claims against the United States. The United States Customs Court was created by Congress to hear cases involving disputes over the levying of custom duties. This court exists by virtue of Congress's power to levy "Duties, Imposts and Excises." There are five justices of the Court of Claims, and they receive $25,500 per annum, while the nine judges of the Customs Court receive $22,500.

Under this same power and its power to grant patents, Congress has created the United States Court of Custom and Patent Appeals. This court hears appeals from the findings of the Customs Court, the Patent Office, and the Tariff Commission. There are five judges whose compensation is $25,500 per annum.

The Tax Court of the United States hears appeals from the findings of the Commissioner of Internal Revenue. There are sixteen members of this court, who serve twelve-year terms and receive a salary of $22,500 per annum.

Under its power to govern territories, Congress has created a

THE STRUCTURE OF THE FEDERAL COURT SYSTEM

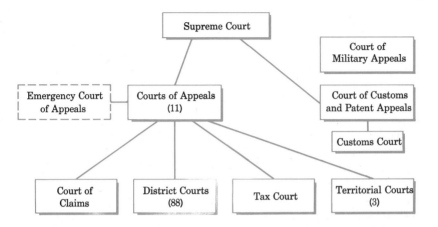

territorial court system. The Supreme Court has said of the territorial courts that: "The jurisdiction with which they are invested is not a part of that judicial power which is defined in the third article of the Constitution, but was conferred by Congress, in the execution of those general powers which that body possesses over the territories of the United States."

United States District Courts have been created for the Canal Zone, Guam, Puerto Rico, and the Virgin Islands. There is a United States District Court for the District of Columbia and also a United States Court of Appeals.

There is also a United States Emergency Court of Appeals, which was created under the Emergency Price Control Act of 1942. Its purpose was to hear appeals from the orders, regulations, and rules of the Price Administrator. This Court continues in existence today under the provisions of the Housing and Rent Control Act of 1948 and the Defense Production Act of 1950. The Chief Justice of the United States designates five justices of the United States Court of Appeals to sit as the Emergency Court of Appeals.

In 1950 Congress created the United States Court of Military Appeals. It consists of three civilians appointed by the President. This court may review convictions by courts-martial under certain conditions and proceedings.

Judicial Power

SECTION 2

The judicial Power shall extend to all Cases, in Law and Equity, arising under this Constitution, the Laws of the United States, and Treaties made, or which shall be made, under their Authority;—to all Cases affecting Ambassadors, other public Ministers and Consuls;— to all Cases of admiralty and maritime Jurisdiction;—to Controversies to which the United States shall be a Party;—to Controversies between two or more States;—between a State and Citizens of another State;— between Citizens of different States;—between Citizens of the same State claiming Lands under Grants of different States, and between a State, or the Citizens thereof, and foreign States, Citizens or Subjects.

In all Cases affecting Ambassadors, other public Ministers and Consuls, and those in which a State shall be Party, the supreme Court shall have original Jurisdiction. In all the other Cases before mentioned, the supreme Court shall have appellate Jurisdiction, both as to Law and Fact, with such Exceptions, and under such Regulations as the Congress shall make.

The Trial of all Crimes, except in Cases of Impeachment, shall be by Jury; and such Trial shall be held in the State where the said Crimes shall have been committed; but when not committed within any State, the Trial shall be at such Place or Places as the Congress may by Law have directed.

The judicial power is the power to decide and "pronounce a judgment and carry it into effect between persons and parties who bring a case before (a court) for decision."

"Judicial power" has also been defined by the Supreme Court as "that power vested in courts to enable them to administer justice according to law."

A case in law is a case which involves an enacted law. An equity case is one in which the court is asked what is fair or right when certain matters involved in the case are not treated by a specific law.

The expression "jurisdiction" refers to the power of a particular court to hear and decide a case. Thus, a federal court can hear cases involving federal laws. A federal case is usually heard first in one of the "inferior courts" established by Congress. Most cases not involving customs, patents, or taxes are heard and decided in a District Court and then a Court of Appeals before being appealed to the Supreme Court for a final decision (see page 146). In such cases the Supreme Court has "appellate jurisdiction." Cases tried in state and local courts can be appealed to the Supreme Court if the issues involved fall within the letter or spirit of the Constitution.

Some cases are heard directly by the Supreme Court without being first tried in a "lower" federal court. These are cases affecting ambassadors and other public officials representing a foreign nation, whether a federal or state law is involved, and cases involving the states. In these cases the Supreme Court has "original jurisdiction."

The judicial power of the United States extends to all cases:

1. Arising under the Constitution and the laws of the United States.
2. Arising under treaties made, or which shall be made, under the authority of the United States.
3. Affecting ambassadors, other public ministers and consuls.
4. Affecting admiralty and maritime matters.
5. Affecting controversies to which the United States shall be a party.
6. Affecting controversies between two or more states.
7. Affecting controversies between a state and citizens of another state. (Action of the United States Supreme Court in accepting jurisdiction of a suit against a state by a citizen of another state in 1793 resulted in such popular reaction that Congress submitted the Eleventh Amendment to the states for ratification. It was speedily adopted, and this section of the Constitution was in effect repealed. Today, a citizen of one state or of a foreign country cannot bring suit against a state in a federal court.)
8. Affecting controversies between citizens of different states, between citizens of the same state claiming lands under grants of different states, and between a state or citizens thereof.

Congress has the power to define the appellate jurisdiction of the Supreme Court, and this it does through the enactment of judicial statutes.

The trial of all crimes against the United States shall be by jury. The only exception is impeachment. By a "crime" is meant not only an offense of a serious nature against a public law of the United States but also, as the United States Supreme Court has stated, "some classes of misdemeanors [petty offenses], the punishment of which involves or may involve the deprivation of the liberty of the citizen." Criminal trials have to be held in the state in which the crime is committed. When the crime is not committed in any state, the trial is held at such place or places as the Congress may direct.

Treason

SECTION 3

Treason against the United States, shall consist only in levying War against them, or in adhering to their Enemies, giving them Aid and Comfort. No Person shall be convicted of Treason unless on the Testimony of two Witnesses to the same overt Act, or on Confession in open Court.

The Congress shall have Power to declare the Punishment of Treason, but no Attainder of Treason shall work Corruption of Blood, or Forfeiture except during the Life of the Person attainted.

This section defines "treason" and provides for its punishment. Only two things constitute "treason" against the United States. One is making war against the United States. The other is giving "Aid and Comfort" to the enemies of the United States. The Constitution also provides that no person can be convicted of treason except on the testimony of two eyewitnesses to the same

150

"overt Act" or on confession in open court. Because tyrants in the past had liquidated their political enemies by charging them with treason because it was undefined, the founders of our government were aware of the dangers attendant to failure to give specific definition to "treason." The requirement of two eyewitnesses to the same "overt Act" was further protection as was the requirement of confession in "open Court." Secret accusations were banished.

No punishment for treason shall fall on anyone except the guilty person. In England the innocent children of those convicted of treason were formerly made to suffer when they were prevented from receiving their inheritance from a guilty parent. Such a condition in America has been prevented by this Article. Congress has the power to determine the punishment for treason, which can be death or a fine and imprisonment depending upon the discretion of the court.

Article IV RELATIONS OF STATES

Public Records

SECTION 1

Full Faith and Credit shall be given in each State to the public Acts, Records, and judicial Proceedings of every other State. And the Congress may by general Laws prescribe the Manner in which such Acts, Records and Proceedings shall be proved, and the Effect thereof.

Acts of the states are made official by having the signatures of the proper authorities and the seals of the state affixed to them. These acts and records must, under this provision of the Constitution, be given full valid recognition by the several states.

Records and judicial proceedings of the courts of any state must be proved or admitted in any other court within the United States by "attestation" of the clerk and the seal of the court, together with a certificate of the judge or magistrate. Such judicial proceedings have such "Faith and Credit" given to them in every court within the United States as they have by law or usage in the courts of the state from which taken.

Rights of an American Citizen in All States

SECTION 2

The Citizens of each State shall be entitled to all Privileges and Immunities of Citizens in the several States.

A Person charged in any State with Treason, Felony, or other Crime, who shall flee from Justice, and be found in another State, shall on Demand of the executive Authority of the State from which he fled, be delivered up, to be removed to the State having Jurisdiction of the Crime.

No Person held to Service or Labour in one State, under the Laws thereof, escaping into another, shall in Consequence of any Law or Regulation therein, be discharged from such Service or Labour, but shall be delivered up on Claim of the Party to whom such Service or Labour may be due.

A citizen from one state going to another state is entitled to all privileges and immunities of the citizens of the state in which he is staying. In other words, this section of the Constitution enables a person to carry with him his rights of state citizenship throughout the Union without embarrassment by state lines. The United States Supreme Court has ruled: "What these fundamental principles are . . . may, however, be all comprehended under the following general heads: protection by the Government; the enjoyment of life and liberty, with the right to acquire and possess property of every kind, and to pursue and obtain happiness and safety, subject nevertheless to such restraints as the Government may justly prescribe for the general good of the whole; the right of a citizen of one State to pass through, or to reside in any other State . . . to claim the benefit of the writ of *habeas corpus;* to institute and maintain actions of any kind in the courts of the State; to take, hold, and dispose of property, either real or personal; and an exemption from higher taxes or impositions than are paid by the other citizens of the State; . . . the elective franchise, as regulated and established by the laws or constitution of the State in which it is to be exercised."

The governor of each state has the duty to deliver up fugitives from justice living in his state who have committed crimes in other states when the governor of those states makes requisition for them. This is called "extradition." This policy of extradition is first found in the provisions of the New England Confederation (see page 32). The duty of a governor to surrender a fugitive is not absolute nor is it unqualified. A federal court cannot compel the governor of one state to surrender a fugitive to another, and on occasion a governor will refuse to do so. For example, the Governor of New Jersey some years ago refused to surrender to Georgia a fugitive from that state's chain-gang system. He remained in New Jersey and became the author of a book entitled *I Am a Fugitive from a Georgia Chain Gang*.

The Constitution also provided for the return of fugitive slaves, but when the Thirteenth Amendment abolished slavery, this clause of the Constitution became obsolete.

Admission of New States

SECTION 3

New States may be admitted by the Congress into this Union; but no new State shall be formed or erected within the Jurisdiction of any other State; nor any State be formed by the Junction of two or more States, or Parts of States, without the Consent of the Legislatures of the States concerned as well as of the Congress.

The Congress shall have Power to Dispose of and make all needful Rules and Regulations respecting the Territory or other Property belonging to the United States; and nothing in this Constitution shall be so construed as to Prejudice any Claims of the United States, or of any particular State.

This section of the Constitution authorizes Congress to admit new states to the Union. All but the original thirteen states were admitted to the Union under this section, Hawaii, the last admitted, being voted by Congress into the Union as the fiftieth state in 1959.

HAWAII STATEHOOD · 1959

Provision is made that a new state cannot be formed from the territory of existing states, either from the territory of one state or several, without the consent of the legislative bodies of the states involved and the permission of Congress. Thus, on February 4, 1791, Congress approved the formation of the State of Kentucky "within the jurisdiction of the Commonwealth of Virginia" after Virginia had agreed to its formation. The states of Tennessee, Maine, and West Virginia were among those added to the Union under this provision governing the formation of states from the territories of other states.

The traditional requirements for statehood are

1. "The inhabitants of the proposed new state are imbued with and are sympathetic toward the principles of democracy as exemplified in the American form of Government."
2. "A majority of the electorate wish statehood."
3. "The proposed new state has sufficient population and resources to support state government and . . . carry its share of the cost of Federal Government."

There are seven main steps in the admission of new states:

1. Petition to Congress for enabling act.
2. Passage of act.
3. Territorial Constitutional Convention.

154

4. Ratification of the State Constitution by the people of the territory.
5. President of the United States must approve the State Constitution.
6. Election of the state officers under provisions of the State Constitution.
7. Proclamation of the President admitting the territory to statehood.

Neither Alaska nor Hawaii waited for an enabling act. Both held Constitutional Conventions and adopted a constitution prior to Congressional action. Congress, in both instances, passed acts accepting their respective constitutions, defined the area of the new states, and delineated the conditions under which Congress would admit the states into the Union. Congress ordered in each case a referendum of the people of each territory on whether they wished to become a state under the conditions set forth in each act. Elections of two United States Senators and one member of Congress was authorized for each of the new states.

All states admitted to the Union are admitted on a basis of equality of constitutional right and power with the "old," or original, states. The unquestionable right of a new state to exercise all the powers of government which the original thirteen states possessed was upheld by the Supreme Court. As soon as a state becomes a member of the Union, its citizens become citizens of the United States on an equal footing with those of the other states.

Congress is given the power to dispose of and make any needed rules or regulations to dispose of the property of the United States.

Congress has the right to act as the local as well as the national governing body of the territories of the United States, since it possesses full sovereignty over territories. Congress has the right to make all the laws and to establish law courts that are needed in these possessions of the Union. Yet, a great degree of self-rule is usually given to a territory so that it has its own legislature elected by the citizens of the territory, and courts of law created by the legislature.

"Republican" Form of Government

SECTION 4

The United States shall guarantee to every State in this Union a Republican Form of Government, and shall protect each of them against Invasion; and on Application of the Legislature, or of the Executive (when the Legislature cannot be convened) against domestic Violence.

Under this clause, the Federal Government guarantees a "Republican Form of Government" to every state and assumes the obligation of protecting each state from invasion and domestic violence.

The Constitution does not define a "Republican Form of Government." The Supreme Court has held that it rests with Congress to determine the republican character of a government in a state. On the grounds that this clause is political rather than judicial, the United States Supreme Court has refused to consider, for example, whether the adoption of the initiative and referendum or the delegation of legislative power to other departments of state government are in keeping with a "Republican Form of Government." By "political" is meant that the political branch of the government—the President and Congress—must make this decision. It is not a matter that can be decided at law. Madison defines a "Republican Form of Government" as "A government which derives all of its powers directly or indirectly from the great body of people, and is administered by persons holding their offices during pleasure, for a limited period, or during good behavior." See discussion on pages 94 ff on the principle of "Republican Form of Government."

In 1895 the United States Supreme Court decided that it is the power and duty of the Federal Government to use the entire strength of the nation "to enforce in any part of the land the full and free exercise of all national powers and the security of all rights entrusted by the Constitution to its care."

Although this section says that a state must be protected against domestic violence "on Application of the Legislature, or of the Executive (when the Legislature cannot be convened)," today the

Federal Government quells domestic violence on the basis, of its power to protect the property of the United States, to remove obstruction to the mails, or to protect interstate commerce, without reference to this constitutional provision. The recent use of federal troops in Arkansas by President Eisenhower has resulted in sharp debate over the constitutionality of his action. The Attorney General of the United States said his action was constitutional, but several authorities on constitutional law contend that President Eisenhower had no congressional or constitutional warrant for his action.

This is based on the argument that the President interfered with the constitutional processes of the state, "first, by enjoining" the Governor of Arkansas "from the exercise of his executive judgment with respect to the National Guard, and, secondly, in failing to call upon the Governor to help provide the necessary deputy marshals to enforce 'judicial process.'"

This was the first time since the Reconstruction Era that a President sent federal troops into a state to prevent violence without the cooperation of the governor of the state or the submission of clear proof of the failure of "judicial process."

Article V   THE AMENDING PROCESS

The Congress, whenever two thirds of both Houses shall deem it necessary, shall propose Amendments to this Constitution, or, on the Application of the Legislatures of two thirds of the several States, shall call a Convention for proposing Amendments, which, in either Case, shall be valid to all Intents and Purposes, as Part of this Constitution, when ratified by the Legislatures of three fourths of the several States, or by Conventions in three fourths thereof, as the one or the other Mode of Ratification may be proposed by the Congress; Provided that no Amendment which may be made prior to the Year One thousand eight hundred and eight shall in any Manner affect the first and fourth Clauses in the Ninth Section of the first Article; and that no State, without its Consent, shall be deprived of its equal Suffrage in the Senate.

This section of the Constitution provides for four methods of adopting amendments to the Constitution:

1. Two-thirds of both Houses of Congress propose the amendment and three-fourths of the state legislatures ratify it.
2. Two-thirds of both Houses of Congress propose the amendment and three-fourths of state conventions ratify it.
3. When the legislatures of two-thirds of the states apply to Congress, Congress "shall" call a National Constitutional Convention to propose amendments and three-fourths of the state legislatures must ratify the amendments.
4. When the legislatures of two-thirds of the states apply to Congress, Congress "shall" call a National Constitutional Convention to propose amendments and three-fourths of state conventions must ratify the amendments.

Only the first two methods have ever been used. Twenty-one of the twenty-two amendments were ratified by the state legislatures. The Twenty-first Amendment, which repealed prohibition, was ratified by state conventions.

It is not probable that the people of the United States will ever employ the calling of a National Constitutional Convention to propose amendments because Congress will submit amendments if there is any widespread demand for them from two-thirds of the states.

The Constitution placed two limitations on the amending process: First, no amendment could be adopted prior to 1808 involving abolition of the slave trade or changing the method of levying a direct tax. This prohibition has long since been obsolete. Second, no state can be deprived of its right to have two Senators by means of an amendment unless a state agrees to such an action.

Article VI SUPREME LAW OF THE LAND

All Debts contracted and Engagements entered into, before the Adoption of this Constitution, shall be as valid against the United States under this Constitution, as under the Confederation.

This Constitution, and the Laws of the United States which shall be made in Pursuance thereof; and all Treaties made, or which shall be made, under the Authority of the United States, shall be the supreme Law of the Land; and the Judges in every State shall be bound thereby, any Thing in the Constitution or Laws of any State to the Contrary notwithstanding.

The Senators and Representatives before mentioned, and the Members of the several State Legislatures, and all executive and judicial Officers, both of the United States and of the several States, shall be bound by Oath or Affirmation, to support this Constitution; but no religious Test shall ever be required as a Qualification to any Office or public Trust under the United States.

The first clause of this article validated all the debts contracted and engagements entered into under the Confederation. This statement gave strength to the credit of the new United States, for it was a pledge to pay the debts incurred under the Confederation.

The second clause provides that the Constitution, the laws of the United States, and all treaties shall be the "supreme Law of the Land." This clause established the supremacy of the Federal Government. Any state constitution or state laws contrary to the Constitution, the treaties, and the laws of the United States cannot be enforced by the federal or state courts. State courts must make their decisions not merely from the state constitution and state laws but "according to the laws and treaties of the United States, 'the supreme Law of the Land'." This second clause of Article VI has been used extensively by the present Supreme Court of the United States in its recent decisions sustaining the pre-emption of a given field of legislation by the Federal Government. In other words, it is now a tenet of American constitutional law that whenever the Federal Government takes exclusively for itself any field of lawmaking, the state governments cannot legislate in that field.

The third clause of Article VI requires all United States Senators, Representatives, members of the several state legislatures, and all executive and judicial officers of both the United States and the several states, to take an Oath or Affirmation to support the Constitution of the United States. On the effect of this clause of the Constitution, Alexander Hamilton wrote: "Thus the legislatures, courts, and magistrates, of the respective members, will be incorporated into the operations of the national government. . . ."

The last clause of this Article forbids that anyone be denied access to an official position with the Federal Government because of his religious beliefs.

Article VII   RATIFICATION

The Ratification of the Conventions of nine States shall be sufficient for the Establishment of this Constitution between the States so ratifying the Same.

This article merely provided that when nine states had ratified, the Constitution would go into operation. For a discussion of the ratification of the Constitution, see pages 75-78.

The Continental Congress on September 13, 1788, directed that the electors of the President be chosen on the first Wednesday in January of 1789, that the electors should vote on the first Wednesday in February, and that the new government begin operations on the first Wednesday in March. George Washington was elected President, and John Adams, Vice President. A quorum did not appear in Congress until April 6, 1789. Washington was inaugurated President on April 30, 1789, in New York City, and the government of the United States of America commenced operations, although the United States Supreme Court did not organize until February 2, 1790.

TOPICAL OUTLINE FOR STUDY

A. Preamble of Constitution
    1. Objectives of the Federal Government
    2. Ordaining and establishing the Constitution
B. Congress
    1. Organization
        (a) Bicameral system
            (i) Senate
            (ii) House of Representatives
        (b) Structure of the Senate
            (i) Original method of electing the United States Senators and reasons for it
            (ii) Present method of electing United States Senators
            (iii) Qualifications of United States Senators
            (iv) Procedure in the Senate
            (v) Privileges and immunities of Senators

4. Miscellaneous powers of Congress
   (a) Naturalization
   (b) Coin money, punish counterfeiters, and fix a standard of weights and measures
   (c) Establish uniform laws on bankruptcy
   (d) Establish post offices
   (e) Grant patents and copyrights
   (f) Constitute tribunals inferior to the Supreme Court
   (g) Define and punish felonies and piracies on the high seas and punish violations of the law of nations
   (h) Exercise exclusive control over a federal district
5. Implied powers of Congress

C. President of the United States
  1. Qualifications of the President
    (a) Residence
    (b) Citizenship
    (c) Age
  2. Method of election
    (a) Political parties
    (b) Presidential primaries
    (c) National political conventions
    (d) Presidential campaign
    (e) National election
    (f) Electoral college
    (g) Congressional canvass of the electoral vote
    (h) Inauguration
  3. Term and compensation
  4. Presidential succession
  5. Immunities of the presidential office
  6. Duties, powers, and responsibilities of the presidential office
    (a) Executive
      (i) Faithful execution of the laws
      (ii) Issuance of rules, regulations, and orders
      (iii) Appointments
      (iv) Removal of officers
      (v) Commissioning of officers of the United States
      (vi) Chief administrator of the government
    (b) Legislative
      (i) Veto
        (α) Veto message
        (β) Pocket veto

        (ii) President's message to Congress on the state of the union
        (iii) Call extra sessions of Congress
    (c) Military
        (i) Commander in chief of the Army and Navy
        (ii) Power over the militia
    (d) Pardoning
        (i) Grant reprieves
        (ii) Grant pardons
    (e) Foreign affairs
        (i) Negotiate treaties with foreign nations
        (ii) Ambassadors and ministers
        (iii) Executive agreements
  7. Vice President
    (a) Presiding officer of the Senate
    (b) Qualifications
    (c) Term and compensation
    (d) Vice President in the scheme of the American government
D. Judiciary
  1. Organization
    (a) Kinds of courts
        (i) United States Supreme Court
        (ii) United States Court of Appeals
        (iii) United States District Courts
        (iv) Special courts
    (b) Personnel of the courts
        (i) Constitutional qualifications for judges
        (ii) Tenure
        (iii) Compensation
        (iv) President's power over the courts through appointments
  2. Jurisdiction of the federal courts
    (a) Original
    (b) Appellate
    (c) Congress' power over the courts through jurisdiction, numbers and compensations
  3. Influence and power of the United States Supreme Court
    (a) Judiciary as a department of government at the time of the foundation of the national government
        (i) Least important of the departments
            (a) Court had not been given the opportunity to settle great contentions and cases

(β) Court had not yet ascertained its own powers and jurisdiction

   (ii) John Jay as the first Chief Justice and his remarks on being offered a re-appointment in 1800

  (b) Power of the Supreme Court to declare acts of Congress unconstitutional

E. Relations to the States
1. Full faith and credit
2. Privileges and immunities of the citizens of one state in another state
3. Extradition
4. Fugitive slaves
5. Establishment of territories
6. Creation of new states
7. Guarantee of republican form of government to every state
8. Protection of a state against domestic violence

F. Amending Process
1. The four methods of amendment
2. The limitations on the amending process

G. Supremacy of National Law
1. Validation of national debt
2. Supreme law of the land
3. Oath of office for public officials

H. Ratification of the Constitution

QUESTIONS

1. What six purposes of the federal government are set forth in the Preamble to the Constitution?
2. Where are all legislative powers under the Constitution vested?
3. What two doctrines of American constitutional law flow from Section 1 of Article I?
4. What are the qualifications of a Representative in Congress?
5. Who decides how many Congressmen there are and when?
6. What were the compromises on slavery in the Constitution?
7. What is the term of office of a Congressman?
8. How are vacancies in the House of Representatives filled?
9. Who chooses the Speaker of the House and its other officers?

10. What branch of Congress has the sole power of impeachment?
11. How many Senators is each state entitled to?
12. Who now elects United States Senators?
13. What is the term of office of a United States Senator?
14. What are the qualifications for a United States Senator?
15. Who is the President of the Senate?
16. When does the Vice President vote in the Senate?
17. Who has the sole power to try all impeachments?
18. What punishment does the Constitution provide for a federal officer who has been removed from office by impeachment?
19. Who determines the time, place, and manner of holding elections for Senators and Representatives?
20. When does Congress assemble and how frequently?
21. What responsibilities does Section 5 of Article I place on the Congress?
22. When may the President call a special session of Congress?
23. What is the monetary compensation for Senators and Representatives?
24. What are the privileges and immunities of a member of Congress?
25. Can a member of Congress hold another public office?
26. Where must revenue bills originate?
27. What four things may the President do with bills passed by Congress?
28. How may Congress get around the presidential veto?
29. List all of the powers which the Constitution vests in Congress.
30. What does "general welfare" mean?
31. Who has complete power over money?
32. What are Congress' war powers?
33. What is the "implied power" clause of the Constitution?
34. What does the Constitution say about slavery?
35. What things is Congress prohibited from doing under Section 9 of Article I?
36. List the limitations on state governments provided by Section 10 of Article I.
37. Summarize the discussion in the Constitutional Convention on the Presidency.
38. How does the electoral college function?
39. Has the House of Representatives ever elected a President?
40. When does the Senate elect a Vice President?
41. Where is the executive power under the Constitution vested?
42. What is the presidential term of office?

43. What are the qualifications for President?
44. What is the presidential succession in case of the death, resignation, or disability of the President?
45. What are the powers and duties of the President?
46. List the President's war powers.
47. Discuss the "executive agreement" as an instrument of foreign policy.
48. Define the presidential power of appointment.
49. What constitutional relationship does the President have to Congress?
50. How may the President, Vice President, and all civil officers of the United States be removed from office?
51. Where does the Constitution vest the "judicial power"?
52. What is the term of office for federal judges?
53. How do federal judges get their offices?
54. What powers over the federal courts does the Constitution give to Congress?
55. What is the history of the number of justices on the Supreme Court?
56. Who creates the courts inferior to the Supreme Court?
57. To what does the judicial power extend under the Constitution?
58. Define the Supreme Court's "original jurisdiction"?
59. What does the Constitution say about trial by jury?
60. Who defines the appellate jurisdiction of the Supreme Court?
61. What is treason against the United States?
62. How may a person be convicted of treason?
63. Who declares the punishment of treason?
64. What does the term "Full Faith and Credit" mean?
65. What are citizens of each state entitled to?
66. What is extradition and how does it work?
67. How may new states be admitted to the Union?
68. Who rules the territories of the United States?
69. Who can dispose of the property of the United States?
70. What is a "Republican Form of Government"? To whom must Congress guarantee this form of government?
71. Does the Constitution authorize the use of federal troops to protect a state against domestic violence?
72. What is the process and procedure of constitutional amendment?
73. How many times have we adopted constitutional amendments by state ratifying conventions?
74. What are the two limitations placed on the "amending process"?

75. Where are all the debts of the Confederation validated by the Constitution?

76. What is the "supreme Law of the Land"?

77. Can a religious test be required as a qualification for holding public office?

78. Does the Constitution require all members of Congress, state legislators, and all executive and judicial officers to take an oath or affirmation to support and defend the Constitution?

79. How many states were required to ratify the Constitution before it could go into operation?

80. When did the first Congress meet?

81. What was the date of Washington's inauguration?

82. When and where did the government under the Constitution commence operations?

CHAPTER 9

The American Bill of Rights

Commenting on the American Bills of Rights, Senator Sumner of Massachusetts once said: "Bills of Rights are lights of political wisdom and anchors of liberty. They are the constant index and also scourge of injustice and wrong." One of the basic reasons for much of the fight over the ratification of the Constitution was due to the fact that the document, as it was submitted for ratification, did not contain a bill of rights.

The friends of the Constitution, under the leadership of James Madison, pledged themselves that in the first Congress of the United States a series of constitutional amendments (a bill of rights) would be submitted for ratification by the states. The first ten amendments to the Constitution of the United States should, therefore, be considered as a part of the same movement which brought into being the Constitution of the United States of America.

Eight of the states that had ratified the Constitution transmitted with their resolutions of ratification a series of suggestions as to what should be included in these amendments. The first Congress

168

received 189 resolutions setting forth what the states considered should be included in the bill of rights. The Congress set to work and prepared for submission to the states twelve amendments to the Constitution on September 25, 1789. The ten amendments that were ratified became operative in December of 1791. There is no record that the states of Connecticut, Georgia, and Massachusetts ever ratified these amendments, which the other states ratified through their state legislatures. The two amendments which failed of ratification would have provided for a reapportionment of representation in Congress and would have fixed the compensation for members of Congress.

The first ten amendments to the Constitution have played an important part as the bulwark for the preservation of the rights of the individual and the rights of the states, hence their importance in our constitutional system. As Justice Frankfurter well put it in a case before him: "the first ten amendments to the Constitution, commonly known as the Bill of Rights, were not intended to lay down any novel principles of government, but simply to embody certain guarantees and immunities which we had inherited from our English ancestors. . . ."

These amendments were originally intended to limit directly and solely the national government, not the states. However, decisions of the United States Supreme Court now hold that all the liberties guaranteed by the "Bill of Rights" are considered as part of the guarantees of "liberty" and "due process" in the Fourteenth Amendment. Hence, these amendments which affect our liberties operate on both state and national governments.

Amendment I FREEDOM OF RELIGION, PRESS, SPEECH, ASSEMBLY, AND PETITION

Congress shall make no law respecting an establishment of religion, or prohibiting the free exercise thereof; or abridging the freedom of speech, or of the press; or the right of the people peaceably to assemble, and to petition the Government for a redress of grievances.

Five Freedoms

The First Amendment guarantees to each individual: first, *freedom of religion;* second, *freedom of speech;* third, *freedom of press;* fourth, *freedom of assembly;* and fifth, *freedom of petition.*

Freedom of Religion

Through its provisions, every person has the full and free privilege of following any religion he wishes as long as the practice of that religion does not violate the recognized common good of all or infringe upon the personal rights of others. Article VI, Section 1, Clause 3, of the Constitution abolished a religious test as a qualification for holding office under the United States Government. In colonial times, there had been a religious qualification for holding office and for the right of franchise. In many of the colonies the church had been supported by taxation. The Federal Government was stopped by this amendment from ever compelling anyone to pay taxes for church support. The basic purpose of this clause was to prevent the establishment of a state church and to prohibit the Federal Government from favoring one religion over another. This amendment made possible the separation of church and state.

Freedom of Speech and of the Press

One of the most vital necessities of free government is freedom of speech and press, both of which are also guaranteed by the First Amendment. In colonial days, Americans had experience with an attempt to suppress freedom of the press in the famous John Peter Zenger case in New York in 1735. This is probably the most famous case involving freedom of press that has ever been tried in an American or English court.

Zenger, an immigrant to America from Germany, had become the publisher of *The New York Weekly Journal.* A dispute over compensation between a former governor, Rip Van Dam, and the new governor, William Crosby, led to the creation of a court of exchequer by Governor Crosby to try the case. The chief justice of New York, Lewis Morris, held that Governor Crosby had no right to create the court for this purpose, whereupon the governor dismissed the chief justice.

Several articles appeared in Zenger's paper siding with Van Dam and Morris. Zenger found himself charged with libel. Van Dam's and Zenger's attorneys were disbarred by the court. Zenger's friends acquired the services of Andrew Hamilton of Philadelphia, whose standing at the bar as the colonies' most famous attorney made it impossible for the court to disbar him.

Ideas and Arguments

Hamilton argued that if the articles were true, they were not a libel, but the court refused to allow presentation of evidence. Hamilton turned to the jury and told them that the suppressing of evidence should be taken as the strongest evidence of the truth of the articles. Hamilton, in an argument with the presiding justice, got him to say to the jury that words constituted a libel according to how they were understood and that they must judge whether these words were libel or not. Holding that speaking the truth was essential to the preservation of the rights of free men, Hamilton closed his case by showing that every free man in the colonies was involved in this case. The jury returned a verdict of not guilty. Prior to this time, all that a jury in a libel or sedition case did was to bring in a verdict that if the *judge* found the publication libelous, the man was guilty. If the *judge* found the publication nonlibelous, then the man was not guilty. Thus the determination of the libel had passed from the judge to the jury. This decision made it impossible to muzzle the colonial press, which later became the vehicle for carrying on the fight against England. Truthfully, Gouverneur Morris once said that the Zenger case "was the morning star of that liberty which subsequently revolutionized America." Freedom of press gained through the Zenger case was to be preserved for all Americans.

Freedom of speech and press does not mean, however, the right to say anything one pleases. A person cannot be slandered and libeled. To preach the overthrow of the government by force is a violation of free speech and press. *A person can advocate a change in government by constitutional amendment, but he becomes a menace to the well-being of every other American when he advocates change by force of arms.* The Supreme Court has said: "the character of every act depends upon the circumstances in which it is done. . . . The most stringent protection of free speech would not protect a man in falsely shouting fire in a theatre and causing a panic. It does not even protect a man from an injunction against uttering words that may have all the effect of force. . . . The question in each case is whether the words are used in such circumstances and are of such nature as to create a clear and present danger that they will bring about the substantive evils that Congress has a right to prevent."

The Supreme Court has also stated that freedom of speech "is nevertheless protected against censorship or punishment, unless shown likely to produce a clear and present danger of a serious substantive evil that rises far above public inconvenience, annoyance, or unrest." This simply means that a person may make any utterance he pleases unless it tends to incite to violence or endangers the foundations of our country. The courts must decide in each instance whether the remarks are seditious or not. The test is whether he who utters them, utters them in such a way as to endanger the nation.

Freedom of Assembly and Petition

Freedom of assembly and petition had been won by Englishmen long before the Constitution. The Supreme Court has said: "The right of the people peaceably to assemble for the purpose of petitioning Congress for a redress of grievances, or for anything else connected with the powers or duties of the national government, is an attribute of national citizenship, and as such under the protection of and guaranteed by the United States. The very idea of a government, republican in form, implies a right on the part of its citizens to meet peaceably for consultation in respect to public affairs and to petition for a redress of grievances."

Amendment II RIGHT TO BEAR ARMS

A well regulated Militia, being necessary to the security of a free State, the right of the people to keep and bear Arms, shall not be infringed.

This amendment guarantees the right to bear arms for the common defense.

Being suspicious of a standing army as a source of danger to a republic, the framers of the Constitution had provided that appropriations for the army should not extend beyond a period of two years (Article I, Section 8). In order to provide for the adequate defense of the country, provision had been made that the militia of the states could be called into the service of the national government. Because of the Second Amendment it would be impossible for the national government to seize all arms in any section of the country, and the states could have a military force to enforce state laws.

Each state can regulate the sale of arms and also make prohibitions against the carrying of concealed weapons as long as these regulations and prohibitions do not interfere with the right to bear arms for the common defense. The U. S. Supreme Court has said that the right of the people "to keep and bear arms is not infringed by laws prohibiting the carrying of concealed weapons."

Amendment III QUARTERING OF TROOPS

No Soldier shall, in time of peace be quartered in any house, without the consent of the Owner, nor in time of war, but in a manner to be prescribed by law.

When we realize that the Declaration of Independence objected to the quartering of armed troops among the colonists, and that in the Petition of Right of 1628 one of the four major points had been a protest against the quartering of troops in private homes without the owner's consent, we can appreciate why the Third Amendment to the Constitution of the United States was insisted upon. This amendment protects the home from military authorities in time of peace and from requisition in time of war except as Congress may authorize by law.

Amendment IV SEARCH AND SEIZURES

The right of the people to be secure in their persons, houses, papers, and effects, against unreasonable searches and seizures, shall not be violated, and no Warrant shall issue, but upon probable cause, supported by Oath or affirmation, and particularly describing the place to be searched, and the persons or things to be seized.

This amendment grew out of the experiences of the colonists with the writs of assistance. The writs of assistance were a sort of general search warrant authorizing an officer to enter and search

174

any place and, upon mere suspicion, to confiscate goods. The Boston merchants in 1760 protested against the issuance of these writs of assistance on the ground that they were unconstitutional. In the course of the trial of the case involving the writs of assistance, James Otis, the American patriot, made his famous plea. He argued that the writs of assistance were unconstitutional and that personal liberty could not be maintained if the government could endanger the life and property of the individual by indiscriminate and unlimited use of the rights of search and seizure. This amendment protects each of us in our persons, homes, papers, and effects against *unreasonable* searches and seizures.

This amendment does not forbid courts from issuing a search warrant that will allow the proper authorities to enter your home to seize property not rightfully possessed by you. The place to be searched must be mentioned in the warrant, along with the articles searched for. Yet an officer of the law may enter and search a house without a warrant when the facts point to a crime having been committed.

This amendment, in protecting your person, forbids the use in a court of law of evidence obtained unlawfully or of confessions secured by the use of force.

Amendment V   RIGHTS OF THE ACCUSED

No person shall be held to answer for a capital, or otherwise infamous crime, unless on a presentment of indictment of a Grand Jury, except in cases arising in the land or naval forces, or in the Militia, when in actual service in time of War or public danger; nor shall any person be subject for the same offence to be twice put in jeopardy of life or limb; nor shall be compelled in any criminal case to be a witness against himself, nor be deprived of life, liberty, or property, without due process of law; nor shall private property be taken for public use, without just compensation.

One of the most important sections of the Constitution is to be found in the Fifth Amendment. Under the provisions of this amendment, no individual can be held for a serious crime except on the *indictment of a grand jury* unless that individual's case arises in the land or naval forces or in the militia when one is actually in service in time of war or public danger. This means that the government cannot make any arbitrary imprisonment.

No person can be put in jeopardy of his life or limb twice for the same offense. If a person is tried in a court of law for a crime and found not guilty, he cannot again be tried for the same crime.

A person cannot be forced to act as a witness against himself in any criminal case.

A witness in any proceeding may refuse to answer any question if his answer might be used against him in a future criminal trial or in uncovering further evidence against him. The witness must explicitly claim his constitutional immunity at the time of the question or he will be presumed to have waived his right. The privilege is a personal one and only applies to an individual.

During 1955-57 there was considerable public discussion and reaction to the "self-incrimination" clause as a result of many witnesses before congressional committees pleading or taking their rights under the Fifth Amendment. Under existing law, witnesses in a federal court, before congressional committees, or before governmental agencies can be given immunity against any prosecution and can be compelled to testify provided the Attorney General is notified and approval of the United States District Court is given.

As Lloyd Wright, former President of the American Bar Association, said in the November 25, 1955, issue of *U.S. News and World Report:* "it seems to me clear that the privilege against self-incrimination conferred by the Fifth Amendment does not, properly construed and limited, so hamper our effort to preserve our way of life that it must be sacrificed or abandoned. The danger lies rather in the intentional misuse and the inadvertent extension of the privilege to mask attempts to destroy the Government."

Life, Liberty, and Property

The most vital part of the Fifth Amendment provides that a person cannot be "deprived of life, liberty, or property without due process of law. . . ." As we have already noted, this right goes back to the Magna Carta of 1215, in which it was provided that no one was to be denied his personal or property rights without the judgment of his peers. By "due process of law" is meant a *fair procedure in a court of law where the law is interpreted in keeping with constitutional limitations.* The "due process of law" clause in the Fifth Amendment applies only against the national government. But in the Fourteenth Amendment it is applied against the state government so that *neither the national nor the state government can deprive a person of life, liberty, or property without the due process of law.* The intent is that each department of government, then, in both the national and in the state sphere of governmental power, must follow the straight path of legal procedure. This is designed to prevent arbitrary and oppressive government. Insofar as humanly possible, the rights of the individual are safeguarded from the arbitrary exercise of the powers of government, and it should be noted that the Fifth Amendment makes no distinction among life, liberty, and property. *If the courts of this nation function according to the Constitution, there can be no arbitrary government in the United States.* As long as each provision in the Fifth Amendment remains unimpaired, there can be no dictatorship in the United States of America.

The amendment also provides that if private property must be taken for public use, it can only be taken after just compensation.

Amendment VI TRIAL BY JURY

In all criminal prosecutions, the accused shall enjoy the right to a speedy and public trial, by an impartial jury of the State and district wherein the crime shall have been committed, which district shall have been previously ascertained by law, and to be informed of the nature and cause of the accusation; to be confronted with the witnesses against him; to have compulsory process for obtaining witnesses in his favor, and to have the Assistance of Counsel for his defence.

The Sixth Amendment guarantees rights with reference to criminal prosecutions by providing that each person accused of a crime is entitled to a *speedy public trial* by an *impartial jury* in the place in which the crime is alleged to have been committed.

Trial by a jury means trial by a jury of twelve citizens. A judge has to be present with power to instruct them on the law. He must also advise them on the facts. The verdict of the jury must be unanimous.

No person can be brought to trial for a crime unless he has first been told of what crime he is accused. Witnesses against him must testify in his presence. The person accused of a crime is guaranteed the legal power of the courts in securing the presence of witnesses he needs, and he is also entitled to a lawyer for his defense, whose fee is paid by the courts if necessary. This, again, is a guarantee against arbitrary trial and imprisonment. Under this section of the Constitution, any person charged with a crime has a chance through the legal process to prove his innocence. Secret trials are thereby forbidden.

Amendment VII TRIAL BY JURY IN CIVIL CASES

In suits at common law, where the value in controversy shall exceed twenty dollars, the right of trial by jury shall be preserved, and no fact tried by a jury, shall be otherwise re-examined in any Court of the United States, than according to the rules of the common law.

The Seventh Amendment provides that in civil suits in common law where the amount of money or the value of goods involved exceeds twenty dollars the right of trial by jury is to be preserved. No case that is tried by jury can be examined in any court of the United States except according to the rules of the common law. The two rules of the common law are, first, that a new trial may be ordered in the courts in which the case originated, and second, that a court of higher jurisdiction can, on a proper writ, review the law involved in the case. This right to jury trial in common law cases can, by mutual agreement of the parties involved, be waived in favor of a trial by a judge.

Amendment VIII LIMITATIONS ON FINES AND PUNISHMENTS

Excessive bail shall not be required, nor excessive fines imposed, nor cruel and unusual punishments inflicted.

Being acquainted with the history of England, the fathers of the Constitution knew what suffering had been caused to men who had earned the displeasure of rulers who imposed excessive bails, fines, and cruel and unusual punishment.

The Eighth Amendment was taken verbatim from one of the provisions of the Bill of Rights that was decreed in the Revolution of 1688.

"Bail" is an amount of money which a person accused of a crime must deposit with the courts if he is to enjoy his liberty before being tried for an offense of which he is accused. The bail he provides is intended to guarantee his appearance in court for his trial. It is returned when he does so.

A judge is restricted in the amount of bail he can set by the provisions of the Eighth Amendment. The Supreme Court has ruled that a bail set so high that a person cannot give bail is to require excessive bail, while another decision held that the ability of the prisoner to give bail and the seriousness of the crime must also be given some consideration. In some cases, such as murder, an accused person is not allowed to give bail.

Concerning cruel and unusual punishments the Supreme Court has ruled that: "if the punishment prescribed for an offence against the laws of the State were manifestly cruel and unusual, as burning at the stake, crucifixion, breaking on the wheel, or the like, it would be the duty of the courts to adjudge such penalties to be within the constitutional prohibition. . . . Punishments are cruel when they involve torture or a lingering death; but the punishment of death is not cruel within the meaning of that word as used in the Constitution."

Amendment IX RIGHTS RETAINED BY THE PEOPLE

The enumeration in the Constitution, of certain rights, shall not be construed to deny or disparage others retained by the people.

Because it had been found impossible to write down in the Constitution all the rights which the people possess, the Ninth Amendment provides that "The people of the United States still keep all those personal rights which they possessed before the Constitution went into effect and which are not specifically mentioned in that document."

Although a traditional right may not be written in the Constitution, that right belongs to the people and cannot be denied to them by the government.

In his book, *The Forgotten Ninth Amendment,* Bennett B. Patterson of the Texas Bar says: "The Ninth Amendment announces and acknowledges in a single sentence that (1) the individual, and not the state, is the source and basis of our social compact and that sovereignty now resides and has always resided in the individual; (2) that our government exists through the surrender by the individual of a portion of his naturally endowed and inherent rights; (3) that everyone of the people of the United States owns a residue of individual rights and liberties which have never been, and which are never to be, surrendered to the State, but which are still to be recognized, protected and secured; and (4) that individual liberty and rights are inherent, and that such rights are not derived from the Constitution, but belong to the individual by natural endowment."

Amendment X POWERS RESERVED TO THE PEOPLE OR THE STATES

The powers not delegated to the United States by the Constitution, nor prohibited by it to the States, are reserved to the States respectively, or to the people.

We have already noted that the Constitution of the United States is a constitution of limited and delegated powers. Under it, Congress is granted certain specific powers. The states are denied certain specific powers. In order that there might not be any question as to where the *undelegated* power of government reposes, the Tenth Amendment was adopted.

The Supreme Court declared that: "Its principal purpose was not the distribution of power between the United States and the States, but a reservation to the people of all powers not granted . . ." to the Federal Government. Thus, the citizens of a state retain the power of meeting the social needs of their community. They can educate their children, provide for the social welfare of the state, and see to the passage and execution of laws required for the functioning of a modern community.

This makes it clear that the Federal Government has only those powers which have been *delegated* to it.

Prior to 1937 the Supreme Court on frequent occasions curtailed the expansion of federal power, particularly in the field of taxation and interstate commerce, by invoking the Tenth Amendment. In the past quarter century, however, the Court has limited the Tenth Amendment on numerous occasions when used in an effort to curtail federal power in the tax, commerce, and other fields. This situation has led Justices Douglas and Frankfurter in their dissenting opinion in a recent case to say: "If the power of the federal government to tax the States is conceded, the reserved power of the States guaranteed by the Tenth Amendment does not give them the independence which they have always been assumed to have."

In 1956 the United States Supreme Court, twice by unanimous vote, declared that when the Federal Government pre-empts any field of lawmaking, the state governments cannot pass laws on the same subject.

According to David Lawrence of the *U.S. News and World Report*: "This is creeping usurpation. It is a denial of the rights which have long protected the States against the tyranny of intolerant majorities in Congress." He claims that this unanimous decision "moved a step nearer to complete erosion of the rights of State sovereignties in America." Legislation introduced during the Eighty-fifth Session of Congress to correct this situation failed of passage. And so the struggle over the interpretation of the Tenth Amendment goes on.

Our Heritage of Liberty

Thus it can be seen how the first ten amendments to the Constitution of the United States constitute the American Bill of Rights. These are restrictions against the exercise by the national government of certain powers which would deny to the individual his right to life, liberty, and property. *The American Bill of Rights has been an active and vital factor in preserving the individual's rights under the common law.* The wisdom of our ancestors in demanding a Bill of Rights has been established beyond any question. The Bill of Rights has been the guardian of the liberties of the American people. Throughout its some 170 years of existence, the Bill of Rights has protected and the government has respected the rights of our citizens.

Today the Constitution of the United States guarantees to every individual twenty-four basic rights. They are

1. Right of the writ of *Habeas Corpus.*
2. Protection against the passage of bills of attainder and *ex post facto laws.*
3. Equality before the law by forbidding the creation of a titled class by prohibiting the federal government from granting titles of nobility.

4. Right to a speedy public trial in case of accusation of crime before an impartial jury at the place of commission of the crime.
5. Freedom of religion, press, speech, assembly, and petition.
6. Right to keep and bear arms for national defense.
7. Protection against the unlawful quartering of troops.
8. Right to grand jury indictment before trial for a crime, and to be confronted with witnesses, and to have the compulsory process to obtain witnesses and the assistance of counsel to establish innocence.
9. Protection against unreasonable searches and seizures.
10. Protection against self-incrimination in any trial or the giving of testimony.
11. Protection against being twice placed in jeopardy of life or limb for crime.
12. Protection against cruel and unusual punishments and excessive bail.
13. Right to just compensation for any property taken for public use.
14. Right to trial by jury in civil cases.
15. Protection against being deprived of life, liberty, or property without due process of law.
16. Protection against the impairment of the obligations of contracts by the states.
17. Equal protection of the laws.
18. Guarantee of a republican form of government in the state in which a citizen resides.
19. Protection from slavery and involuntary servitude except as punishment for crime. (See page 190.)
20. Protection from abridgement by the states of the privileges and immunities of citizens of the United States. (See page 192.)
21. Right to hold public office under the United States if the citizen meets the statutory and constitutional qualifications.
22. Right to freedom of ingress and egress from a state.
23. Protection from domestic violence and foreign invasion.
24. Protection from the abridgment of the right to vote by a state on account of race or sex. (See page 198.)

These rights are the basis and foundation of the liberty that we enjoy in the United States of America today.

TOPICAL OUTLINE FOR STUDY

A. Demand for an American Bill of Rights
B. First Amendment
    1. Freedom of religion
    2. Freedom of speech
    3. Freedom of press
    4. Freedom of assembly
    5. Freedom of petition
C. Second Amendment
D. Third Amendment
E. Fourth Amendment
    1. Search warrants
    2. Seizures
F. Fifth Amendment
    1. Indictment of grand jury
    2. Double jeopardy
    3. Life, liberty, and property
G. Sixth Amendment
    1. Speedy public trial
    2. Impartial jury
    3. Guarantees against arbitrary trial and imprisonment
H. Seventh Amendment
    1. Right of trial by jury in suits in common law
    2. The rules of common law
I. Eighth Amendment
J. Ninth Amendment
K. Tenth Amendment
L. Bill of Rights in the Preservation of the Rights of the Individual

QUESTIONS

1. What did Senator Sumner of Massachusetts say about the Bill of Rights?
2. How was the Bill of Rights added to the Constitution?
3. Does the Bill of Rights limit the federal or the state governments? Explain your answer.
4. What does the First Amendment guarantee to each individual?
5. Who was John Peter Zenger, and what is his significance in American history?
6. Does freedom of speech and press carry with it the right to say anything one pleases? Explain.
7. What has the United States Supreme Court said on freedom of assembly and petition?
8. What does the Second Amendment guarantee? Why was it necessary?
9. What is the significance of the Third Amendment?
10. Why was the Fifth Amendment incorporated into the Constitution?
11. What is the significance of the "self-incrimination" clause of the Fifth Amendment?
12. Explain fully the provisions of the Fifth Amendment. Why are they vital to you?
13. Which of the first ten amendments gives to an accused individual the chance through legal process to prove his innocence?
14. What guarantees are contained in the Seventh Amendment?
15. What does the Eighth Amendment prohibit?
16. What particular significance is attached to the Ninth Amendment?
17. Why is the Tenth Amendment today one of the most important sections of our Constitution?
18. What are the twenty-four basic rights which the Constitution of the United States guarantees today to every citizen?

1913 1913

1870 1919

1868 1920

1865 1933

1804 1933

1798 1951

CHAPTER **10**

The Eleventh to the Twenty-Third Amendment

Amendment XI SUITS AGAINST STATES

The Judicial power of the United States shall not be construed to extend to any suit in law or equity, commenced or prosecuted against one of the United States by Citizens of another State, or by Citizens or Subjects of any Foreign State.

The Constitution provided that the federal courts should have power to hear cases "between a State and Citizens of another State; . . . (Article III, Section 2, Clause 1)." States regarded themselves as sovereigns, and there had been an old theory that the sovereign could not be sued. Hence the states objected because they felt that their sovereignty was weakened if citizens of another state could sue them.

In the case of Chisholm v. Georgia, the whole matter came to a

187

head before the United States Supreme Court in 1793. Georgia contended that the Court had no right to hear the case because the Constitution conferred jurisdiction only to the federal courts when a state brought suit against the citizens of another state. The Court overruled this argument and said that it could hear a case of this nature even if it were brought by a citizen of one state against another state.

The decision raised a storm of protest from the states, and Congress submitted an amendment taking away from the federal courts all power to hear a case involving a state and the citizens of another state or between an alien and a state. The Eleventh Amendment became a part of the Constitution on January 8, 1798. If a citizen of another state or a foreign nation desires to institute a suit against a state, he must do so in the courts of that state under the provisions of the laws of that state.

Amendment XII ELECTION OF PRESIDENT AND VICE-PRESIDENT

The Electors shall meet in their respective states and vote by ballot for President and Vice-President, one of whom, at least, shall not be an inhabitant of the same state with themselves; they shall name in their ballots the person voted for as President, and in distinct ballots the person voted for as Vice-President, and they shall make distinct lists of all persons voted for as President, and of all persons voted for as Vice-President, and of the number of votes for each, which lists they shall sign and certify, and transmit sealed to the seat of the government of the United States, directed to the President of the Senate;—The President of the Senate shall, in the presence of the Senate and House of Representatives, open all the certificates and the votes shall then be counted;—The person having the greatest number of votes for President shall be the President, if such number be a majority of the whole number of Electors appointed; and if no person have such majority, then from the persons having the highest numbers not exceeding three on the list of those voted for as President, the House of Representatives shall choose immediately, by ballot, the President. But in choosing the President, the votes shall be taken by states, the representation from each state having one vote; a quorum for this purpose shall consist of a member or members

from two-thirds of the states, and a majority of all the states shall be necessary to a choice. And if the House of Representatives shall not choose a President whenever the right of choice shall devolve upon them, before the fourth day of March next following, then the Vice-President shall act as President, as in the case of the death or other constitutional disability of the President.—The person having the greatest number of votes as Vice-President, shall be the Vice-President, if such number be a majority of the whole number of Electors appointed, and if no person have a majority, then from the two highest numbers on the list, the Senate shall choose the Vice-President; a quorum for the purpose shall consist of two-thirds of the whole number of Senators, and a majority of the whole number shall be necessary to a choice. But no person constitutionally ineligible to the office of the President shall be eligible to that of Vice-President of the United States.

The Twelfth Amendment was adopted to correct a defect in the method of electing the President and Vice President of the United States. We have already noted that the Constitution (Article II, Section 1, Clause 3) provided that the electoral college was to vote for two persons, *not* indicating which was its choice for President and which for Vice President. In the election of 1800, because of this provision, there was a tie between Burr and Jefferson. The electors had meant to elect Jefferson President and Burr Vice

189

President, but the Constitution did not allow them to make this designation on their ballots. It became obvious that if all electors belonging to the successful party voted for the same two candidates, there would always be a tie vote. The Twelfth Amendment, requiring that the electors should vote for President on one ballot and for Vice President on another ballot, corrected this difficulty when it became part of the Constitution on September 25, 1804.

Amendment XIII   SLAVERY

Slavery Abolished

SECTION 1

Neither slavery nor involuntary servitude, except as a punishment for crime whereof the party shall have been duly convicted, shall exist within the United States, or any place subject to their jurisdiction.

Power of Congress

SECTION 2

Congress shall have power to enforce this article by appropriate legislation.

The Thirteenth, Fourteenth, and Fifteenth Amendments to the Constitution were the direct result of the War Between the States. The Constitution, as we have already seen, recognized slavery as a legal institution. However, nowhere in the Constitution was the word "slave" or "slavery" used.

Under Section 9 of Article I, the federal government was prohibited from stopping the importation of slaves until 1808.

One of the compromises of the Constitution provided that only three-fifths of the slaves would be counted for purposes of representation or taxation. Article IV, Section 2, Clause 3, of the Constitution provided for the return of fugitive slaves.

In 1787, the Congress of the Confederation passed the Northwest Ordinance, which abolished slavery north of the Ohio River in the Northwest Territory. (This made free states of Michigan, Wisconsin, Illinois, Indiana, and Ohio.) In the first three decades of our history, the balance between the North and the South was maintained by admitting into the Union first a free state and then a slave state. Thus the area between the Atlantic and the Mississippi was divided in a friendly way between nonslavery and slavery. When we acquired the Louisiana Purchase, nothing was said about division between slave and nonslave states. Under these circumstances the South felt it had the right to extend slavery into this area. Accordingly, in March of 1818 Missouri sought admission into the Union as a slave state, but Congress failed to admit Missouri in 1818 and again in 1819. Violent emotional debate in Congress and in the nation as a whole forced Congress to seek a compromise. There were eleven free states and eleven slave states in the Union at the time, when Maine sought admission as a free state. This circumstance suggested the Missouri Compromise of 1820, whereby both Missouri and Maine were admitted to the Union. The Compromise prohibited slavery north of 36° 30′ north latitude in the rest of the Louisiana Purchase. The balance between free states and slaves states was maintained.

Controversy "reared its head" again after the acquisition of new territory after the Mexican War. The extension of the line of 36° 30′ would have satisfied the South, but the North was now determined to stop the further extension of slavery into the territories of the United States. When California sought admission as a free state, the debate started all over again. It was settled by the Compromise of 1850, which admitted California as a free state and gave the North control of the Senate. The territories of New Mexico and Utah were created without any restriction as to slavery. There were other concessions made to both the North and South. The struggle between the proslavery and antislavery forces over Kansas helped bring on the War Between the States.

Just after the Battle of Bull Run in 1861, Congress passed a resolution to the effect that the North was not seeking to interfere with the institution of slavery but merely seeking to preserve the Union. Within a year, public opinion in the North forced the reversal of that position. The Confiscation Act of 1862 offered freedom to the slaves of persons who were resisting the Union. President Lincoln, as a war measure, issued the Emancipation Proclamation on September 23, 1862, effective January 1, 1863. This freed all the slaves in those areas of the United States still in open insurrection against the United States.

In his annual message of December 1, 1863, President Lincoln

advocated a constitutional amendment freeing the slaves. The amendment was introduced on March 28, 1864, and was submitted to the states on January 31, 1865. On December 18, 1865, it was declared part of the Constitution.

This amendment abolished slavery, peonage, and all forms of involuntary servitude except as punishment for a crime. A resident could be drafted for military service. Mexican peonage and Chinese coolie labor are reached by this amendment as the United States Supreme Court made very clear in the Slaughter House Cases: "It reaches every race and every individual, and if in any respect it commits one race to the nation, it commits every race and every individual thereof. Slavery or involuntary servitude of the Chinese, of the Italian, of the Anglo-Saxon are as much within its compass as slavery or involuntary servitude of the African."

Amendment XIV **LIMITATIONS ON THE STATES**
Civil Rights
SECTION 1

All persons born or naturalized in the United States, and subject to the jurisdiction thereof, are citizens of the United States, and of the State wherein they reside. No State shall make or enforce any law which shall abridge the privileges or immunities of citizens of the United States; nor shall any State deprive any person of life, liberty, or property, without due process of law; nor deny to any person within its jurisdiction the equal protection of the laws.

Apportionment of Representatives
SECTION 2

Representatives shall be apportioned among the several States according to their respective numbers, counting the whole number of persons in each State, excluding Indians not taxed. But when the right to vote at any election for the choice of electors for President and Vice President of the United States, Representatives in Congress, the Executive and Judicial officers of a State, or the members of the Legislature thereof, is denied to any of the male inhabitants of such State, being twenty-one years of age, and citizens of the United States, or in any way abridged, except for participation in rebellion, or other crime, the basis of representation therein shall be reduced in the proportion which the number of such male citizens shall bear to the whole number of male citizens twenty-one years of age in such State.

Political Disabilities
SECTION 3

No person shall be a Senator or Representative in Congress, or elector of President and Vice President, or hold any office, civil or military, under the United States, or under any State, who, having previously taken an oath, as a member of Congress, or as an officer of the United States, or as a member of any State Legislature, or as an executive or judicial officer of any State, to support the Constitution of the United States, shall have engaged in insurrection or rebellion against the same, or given aid or comfort to the enemies thereof. But Congress may by a vote of two-thirds of each House, remove such disability.

Public Debt
SECTION 4

The validity of the public debt of the United States, authorized by law, including debts incurred for payment of pensions and bounties for services in suppressing insurrection or rebellion, shall not be questioned. But neither the United States nor any State shall assume

*or pay any debt or obligation incurred in aid of insurrection or re-
bellion against the United States, or any claim for the loss or emancipation of any slave; but all such debts, obligations and claims shall
be held illegal and void.*

Power of Congress

SECTION 5

*The Congress shall have power to enforce, by appropriate legisla-
tion, the provisions of this article.*

The Fourteenth Amendment grew out of President Johnson's
attitude toward the Civil Rights Bill which he vetoed and from
the recommendation of the Joint Congressional Committee on
Reconstruction. The Committee advocated that the main provisions of the Civil Rights Bill be written into the Constitution.
Congress passed the Fourteenth Amendment on June 13, 1866.

There was considerable controversy over its ratification since
ratification was made a condition for the readmission of the Confederate States. On July 21, 1868, Congress passed a joint resolution declaring that twenty-nine states (twenty-eight being required) had ratified and ordered Secretary of State Seward to declare it a part of the Constitution. Seward did this on July 28,
1868.

Civil rights during the past ten years have come in for considerable public discussion. Both the Republican and Democratic
platforms of 1944, 1948, 1952, and 1956 contained civil rights
planks. President Truman recommended civil rights legislation
without success during his term of office. In 1956 President Eisenhower recommended a bipartisan civil rights commission, and in
1957 he pressed for enactment of a law.

A Civil Rights Act, the first since 1875, was passed by Congress
on August 29, 1957. The legislation was requested by President
Eisenhower. Certain basic provisions asked by the Administration
were eliminated: for example, the provision authorizing the President to use troops to enforce civil rights laws was defeated in the
Senate.

The Civil Rights Act of 1957 created a Commission on Civil
Rights consisting of six persons, not more than three from the

same political party. These Commissioners are appointed by the President with the advice and consent of the Senate. This act vests the Commission with the authority to investigate any allegations that United States citizens are deprived of their right to vote by reason of color, race, religion, or national origin. It also directs the Commission to study and investigate the denial of equal protection of the laws. The Commission was given a full-time staff Director, appointed by the President with the advice and consent of the Senate.

Under the terms of the bill a new Civil Rights Divisions was created in the Department of Justice under an Assistant Attorney General. The jurisdiction of the United States District Courts was extended to include any civil action to secure damages or relief from violation of any provisions of the Civil Rights Act. Among the things prohibited by the act are any attempts to "intimidate or coerce" persons from voting. The Attorney General is empowered to seek an injunction to stop such attempts. The penalties for those found guilty of violating civil rights provide a fine of not more than $1000 and/or a prison term not to exceed six months.

On July 18, 1957, Senator Javits of New York presented to Congress a statement prepared by the Department of Justice listing the following as the civil rights involved under the Civil Rights Act of 1957 (as reported by *Congressional Quarterly*):

1. "Right to vote in Federal elections.
2. Right of a voter in a Federal election to have his ballot fairly counted.
3. Right to vote in all elections, free from discrimination by states on account of race or color.
4. Right to inform a Federal officer of a violation of Federal law.
5. Right to testify in Federal court.
6. Right to be free from mob violence while in Federal custody.
7. Right to be secure from unlawful searches and seizures.
8. Right to peaceably assemble free from unreasonable restraint by state or local officials.
9. Freedom of religion.
10. Freedom of speech and of the press.

11. Right not to be purposefully discriminated against in public employment on account of race or color.
12. Right not to be denied use or enjoyment of any Government-operated facilities on account of race or color.
13. Right not to be segregated under compulsion of state authority on account of race or color.
14. Right not to be denied due process of law or equal protection of the law in other regards.
15. Right to be free to perform a duty imposed by the Federal Constitution.
16. Right, when charged with a crime, to a fair trial.
17. Right not to be tried by ordeal or summarily punished other than in the manner prescribed by law.
18. Right not to be forced to confess an offense.
19. Right to be free from brutality at the hands of prison officials.
20. Right to representation by counsel at criminal trial.
21. Right to trial by a jury from which members of the defendant's race have not been purposely excluded.
22. Right of prisoner to protection by officer having him in custody.
23. Right not to be held in peonage.
24. Right not to be held in slavery or involuntary servitude."

During the first session of the Eighty-sixth Congress (1959), President Eisenhower submitted a seven-point program on civil rights. According to *Congressional Quarterly* the features were as follows:

1. "An anti-mob bill, making interference with a Federal-court school desegregation order a Federal crime.
2. An anti-bombing bill, making it a Federal crime to cross state lines to avoid prosecution for bombing a school or church.
3. A bill to give the Justice Department the right to inspect voting records and requiring the preservation of those records.
4. Extension of the life of the Civil Rights Commission.
5. A bill to give statutory authority to the President's Committee on Government Contracts, which seeks to eliminate discrimination in private employment.

6. A bill authorizing limited technical and financial aid to areas faced with school desegregation problems.
7. Provision of emergency schooling for armed forces children in event public schools are closed by integration disputes."

Congress did not go along with the President's program. It extended the life of the Civil Rights Commission for a period of two years.

The Fourteenth Amendment to the Constitution is as important as the Fifth Amendment because it contains the "due process of law" clause made applicable against the states. The Fourteenth Amendment makes *all* persons *born* or *naturalized* in the United States *citizens of the United States and of the state in which they live*. No state is allowed to make any law that would abridge the privileges and immunities of citizens of the United States. Under the Constitution no person can be deprived by the state of life, liberty, or property without the due process of law. Each person must have the *equal protection of the laws* in the state.

The amendment abolished the three-fifths compromise in apportioning the number of Representatives in the House (see Article I, Section 2, Clause 3) and provides that if any male citizen over twenty-one years of age is denied the right to vote, the state's representation in Congress will be reduced accordingly.

Any person who had held an office under the United States or a state and had sworn to support and protect the Constitution, and then had participated in the rebellion against the Union, was excluded from public office, subject to congressional removal of the disability. These restrictions were finally removed by Congress in 1898.

The amendment outlawed all the debts incurred by the Confederacy and the Confederate States in fighting the War Between the States. It forbade the payment of any claim for the loss or emancipation of slaves. The validity of the public debt of the United States incurred by the Union was recognized as unquestioned.

The "equal protection" clause of the Fourteenth Amendment has been a matter of current discussion. From the adoption of the Fourteenth Amendment to recent times the requirements of the "equal protection" clause were met by providing separate but equal facilities. In 1896 the United States Supreme Court in the Plessy v. Ferguson case found this type of segregation to be constitutional. This was the "law of the land" until 1954, when the United States Supreme Court in a unanimous opinion forbade the continuance of segregation in the field of public education.

Amendment XV   RIGHT TO VOTE

Right of Negroes to Vote

SECTION 1

The right of citizens of the United States to vote shall not be denied or abridged by the United States or by any State on account of race, color, or previous conditions of servitude.

Power of Congress

SECTION 2

The Congress shall have power to enforce this article by appropriate legislation.

The Fifteenth Amendment became part of the Constitution on March 30, 1870, prohibiting the Federal Government and the states from denying to any citizen the right to vote because of his race, color, or previous condition of servitude. It should be noted that this amendment does not give the right to vote to anybody. Determination of qualifications of voters is left wholly in the hands of the states.

Amendment XVI   INCOME TAX

The Congress shall have power to lay and collect taxes on incomes, from whatever source derived, without apportionment among the several States, and without regard to any census or enumeration.

The Sixteenth Amendment provides for the levy of a direct federal tax on incomes without the need of taxing the citizens of states according to a division of the tax based on the population of states (Article I, Section 2, Clause 3).

A federal income tax was passed during the War Between the

States in 1862 as a war measure in order to raise a portion of the revenue necessary to carry on the war. This law taxed incomes of over $600 per annum and established a progressively increasing rate on the amounts over $600.

In 1870 a case involving the constitutionality of the income tax during the War Between the States was decided by the United States Supreme Court. In this case, Springer v. United States, the Supreme Court held that the income tax was "within the category of an excise duty," not a direct tax and, therefore, was constitutional. In other words, Congress had the power to pass it without apportioning it on a population basis. In 1872 this income tax was allowed to expire.

In 1894 a second income tax was passed as a result of the Populist platform in the presidential election of 1892, which had declared emphatically in favor of a national income tax. In the election of 1892, the Populists, who were strong particularly in the middle western part of the United States, succeeded in electing a number of United States Senators and Representatives. The income tax bill of 1894 was a rider to the Tariff Bill of that year. A case was taken to the Supreme Court contesting the constitutionality of the Act of 1894. The Supreme Court reversed its findings in the Springer case, and in the case of Pollock v. Farmers' Loan and Trust Company held that the income tax was a direct tax and unconstitutional because it was not levied in proportion to the census.

Unlimited Taxation

As a result of this decision, in 1895, there followed a gradually increasing agitation under the leadership of the Populists to amend the Constitution of the United States. Finally, on July 12, 1909, Congress passed a joint resolution submitting this amendment to the state legislatures for ratification. It took three and one-half years to ratify the Sixteenth Amendment. On February 25, 1913, the amendment became a part of the Constitution. It gave the power of *unlimited income taxation* to the Federal Government.

Amendment XVII POPULAR ELECTION OF UNITED STATES SENATORS

(1) The Senate of the United States shall be composed of two Senators from each State, elected by the people thereof, for six years; and each Senator shall have one vote. The electors in each State shall have the qualifications requisite for electors of the most numerous branch of the State legislatures.

(2) When vacancies happen in the representation of any State in the Senate, the executive authority of such State shall issue writs of election to fill such vacancies: Provided, That the legislature of any State may empower the executive thereof to make temporary appointments until the people fill the vacancies by election as the legislature may direct.

(3) This amendment shall not be so construed as to affect the election or term of any Senator chosen before it becomes valid as part of the Constitution.

The Seventeenth Amendment to the Constitution provides for the *popular election of United States Senators*. From the discussion of the Constitutional Convention, page 77, you will recall that there was considerable debate as to the method by which the Senators were to be chosen. At one time or another, recommendations were considered which would have resulted in presidential appointment of Senators, in their direct election by the people, in their election by the members of the House of Representatives, and in the method that actually became a part of the Constitution—the election of Senators by state legislatures (Article I, Section 3, Clause 1).

But many undesirable conditions were encouraged under this method of electing Senators. Often the state legislatures had trouble reaching a majority decision on the election of a Senator, delaying the important business of their states through the long time spent electing a Senator. Then, too, there were charges of bribery in connection with the elections, some men even being elected to the state legislature mainly on their promise to vote for a certain man for Senator.

The argument was advanced that the election of United States Senators by legislatures was undemocratic and that direct election was more in keeping with the spirit of the people.

In 1893 the House of Representatives passed a resolution submitting a constitutional amendment for the popular election of United States Senators, but the Senate voted it down. Between 1894 and 1904 the House of Representatives passed a resolution on five different occasions submitting such a proposed constitutional amendment; but on all five occasions the Senate rejected the amendment.

In 1892 and 1896 the Populist party came out with platforms in favor of the amendment. Then the Democratic party in 1900 endorsed it, and in 1908 William Howard Taft, the Republican nominee, pronounced himself in favor of popular election. By 1912, twenty-nine states were already, in effect, electing United States Senators by direct vote of the people. Congress submitted the constitutional amendment for ratification on June 12, 1911; and it was proclaimed as a part of the Constitution on May 31, 1913.

Amendment XVIII   PROHIBITION

Prohibition of Intoxicating Liquors

SECTION 1

After one year from the ratification of this article the manufacture, sale, or transportation of intoxicating liquors within, the importation thereof into, or the exportation thereof from the United States and all territory subject to the jurisdiction thereof for beverage purposes is hereby prohibited.

Enforcement

SECTION 2

~~The Congress and the several States shall have concurrent power to enforce this article by appropriate legislation.~~

Ratification

SECTION 3

~~This article shall be inoperative unless it shall have been ratified as an amendment to the Constitution by the legislatures of the several States, as provided in the Constitution, within seven years from the date of the submission hereof to the States by the Congress.~~

Prohibition came to America after nearly a century of agitation. The first organized movement against alcoholic drink started in Boston as early as 1826 with the organization of temperance societies. The first state prohibition law in American history was passed by Maine in 1846. In 1851 the Society of Good Templars was founded to bring about temperance and prohibition. This organization was the forerunner of the National Prohibition Party and of the Women's Christian Temperance Union.

During the War Between the States liquor taxes were a very substantial source of revenue, and following the war there was a substantial increase in the liquor business of the country. This led to agitation against the use of intoxicants, and those believing in prohibition charged that the liquor interests were a nefarious influence on politics.

In May, 1869, some 500 delegates representing twenty states came to Chicago to found the National Prohibition Party. The party presented its first candidates for President and Vice President in the election of 1872. The party never succeeded in mustering much support for its candidates at the polls, although it remains to this day as a party.

Under the leadership of Frances E. Willard the Women's Christian Temperance Union was organized in 1874. In 1893 the American Anti-Saloon League came into being. These two organizations were dominant forces in bringing prohibition to the United States. The Anti-Saloon League maintained a powerful lobby in

Washington and in most state capitols. It turned out its own newspapers and literally millions of pamphlets and various prohibition literature. It endorsed and opposed candidates for public office. World War I put the country on its way to prohibition when the Food Control Act was passed, prohibiting the use of food materials in the production of distilled beverages and putting severe restrictions on the making of malt and vinous liquors. The National Emergency Agricultural Appropriation Act provided for wartime prohibition.

Prior to this action, some fourteen states were legally dry and many other states operated under local option laws.

Andrew Volstead

Attempts to pass a constitutional amendment dated back to 1876. Congress passed the Eighteenth Amendment on December 18, 1917, which prohibited the sale, manufacture, and transportation of intoxicating liquor for beverage purposes. The amendment became operative on January 16, 1920. Congress, urged on by Andrew Volstead, passed the Volstead Act to place the amendment into operation. This act defined intoxicating liquor as any beverage which contained more than one-half of one percent of alcohol. The Volstead Bill was first vetoed by President Wilson, but Congress repassed it over his veto. Our national experiment with prohibition did not succeed. The bootlegging business was taken over by gangsters, and the attitude of the American people toward prohibition slowly began to change. Enforcement posed very serious problems, and the result was the repeal of the amendment.

The Eighteenth Amendment was the first amendment submitted by Congress that ever contained a clause in it setting a limit within which the states must ratify an amendment. If, within seven years, the requisite number of states failed to ratify, then the amendment was dead. The Twenty-first Amendment, adopted in 1933, repealed the Eighteenth Amendment and provided that "the transportation or importation into any State, Territory, or Pos-

session of the United States for delivery or use therein of intoxicating liquors, in violation of the laws thereof, is hereby prohibited." Thus the Federal Government must see that its regulation of interstate commerce shall not render state prohibition laws
ineffective wherever they may exist. The Twenty-first Amendment
is the only amendment in our history ratified by state conventions.

Amendment XIX   WOMAN SUFFRAGE

*The right of citizens of the United States to vote shall not be
denied or abridged by the United States or by any State on account
of sex.*

*Congress shall have power to enforce this article by appropriate
legislation.*

An amendment to the Constitution recognizing the right of
women to vote was first advocated in 1869. It is said that woman
suffrage agitation first started while Jackson was President. In
1838 Kentucky gave the women the right to vote in school-board
elections. Several other states subsequently did the same. In 1887
Kansas permitted women to vote in municipal elections. Wyo-
ming, as a territory in 1869, gave the women equal voting rights
with men and became the first state with woman suffrage when
admitted to the Union in 1890.

The fight for a constitutional amendment commenced when
Congress passed the Fifteenth Amendment. The Suffragettes were
disappointed that there was no provision made in the amendment
for woman suffrage. The women continued an unrelenting battle
for the right to vote, employing suffragette parades and other mili-
tant measures to dramatize their cause. Among the famous women
leaders in the struggle for woman suffrage were Lucretia Mott,
Elizabeth Stratton, Lucy Stone, and Susan B. Anthony. By 1918
fifteen states had granted equal suffrage to women.

In 1918 President Wilson, who had previously been opposed to
woman suffrage, recommended to Congress that a constitutional
amendment be submitted to the states. The great work done by
the women in World War I had convinced many people they were
entitled to voting rights.

This amendment, ratified on August 26, 1920, granted women the right to vote by providing that the right to vote could not be abridged by the United States or any state on account of sex.

Amendment XX THE LAME DUCK AMENDMENT

Terms of President and Vice-President

SECTION 1

The terms of the President and Vice-President shall end at noon on the 20th day of January, and the terms of Senators and Representatives at noon on the 3d day of January, of the years in which such terms would have ended if this article had not been ratified; and the terms of their successors shall then begin.

Meetings of Congress

SECTION 2

The Congress shall assemble at least once in every year, and such meeting shall begin at noon on the 3d day of January, unless they shall by law appoint a different day.

Acting President

SECTION 3

If, at the time fixed for the beginning of the term of the President, the President elect shall have died, the Vice-President elect shall become President. If a President shall not have been chosen before the time fixed for the beginning of his term, or if the President elect shall have failed to qualify, then the Vice-President elect shall act as President until a President shall have qualified; and the Congress may by law provide for the case wherein neither a President elect nor a Vice-President elect shall have qualified, declaring who shall then act as President, or the manner in which one who is to act shall be selected, and such person shall act accordingly until a President or Vice-President shall have qualified.

Choice of President by Congress

SECTION 4

The Congress may by law provide for the case of the death of any of the persons from whom the House of Representatives may choose a President whenever the right of choice shall have devolved upon them, and for the case of the death of any of the persons from whom the Senate may choose a Vice-President whenever the right of choice shall have devolved upon them.

Time of Effect

SECTION 5

Sections 1 and 2 shall take effect on the 15th day of October following the ratification of this article.

Ratification

SECTION 6

This article shall be inoperative unless it shall have been ratified as an amendment to the Constitution by the legislature of three-fourths of the several States within seven years from the date of its submission.

The Twentieth Amendment to the Constitution, ratified in 1933, caused "lame duck" Congresses to be eliminated and advanced the date of the inauguration of the President of the United States.

The term "lame ducks" refers to those members of Congress who had been defeated for re-election, but who, because of a special circumstance, would not lose their representation in Congress until five months after they were defeated. How did this condition come about? The Constitution does not declare when the terms of Senators and Representatives are to begin, but does determine their term of office (six years for a Senator and two years for a Representative). The Continental Congress in September, 1788, passed an act "that the first Wednesday in March next be the time for commencing proceedings under the Constitution." This day was March 4, and it remained as the day on which the term of office of members of Congress began. To change that date would change the term of office of those members in office when such a change occurred.

Now the first session of Congress was scheduled for the first Monday in December (Article I, Section 4, Clause 2). Members of Congress elected in November could not assume their duties until the following December unless the President called a special session of Congress after the March 4 on which the newly elected members officially took office. During the "short session" between the first Monday in the December immediately after the election and March 4, the defeated members of Congress could pass or veto laws, yet they would not be the latest chosen representatives of the people. The Twentieth Amendment changed this condition.

It provides that the terms of the President and Vice President of the United States shall terminate on January 20 instead of March 4. The terms of United States Senators and Representatives shall terminate on January 3. Congress is to assemble once each year on January 3, unless Congress by law provides for another date.

If the President elect dies before his inauguration, the Vice-President elect shall become President.

If a President is not chosen before January 20 or if the President elect fails to qualify, the Vice-President elect shall act as President until a President shall have qualified.

Congress is given the power to provide by law for the case

wherein neither a President elect nor a Vice-President elect shall have qualified. It also has the power to declare who shall act as President or the manner in which one who is to act shall be selected.

Under this provision of the Twentieth Amendment, Congress passed the Presidential Succession Act of 1948. Under the act, the succession to the Presidency passes from the Vice President to the Speaker of the House, to the President pro tempore of the Senate and, finally, to the members of the Cabinet in the order of the establishment of their departments.

Up to now, the succession has never had to go beyond the Vice President.

Amendment XXI   REPEAL OF PROHIBITION

Statement of Repeal

SECTION 1

The eighteenth article of amendment to the Constitution of the United States is hereby repealed.

Transportation or Importation of Liquor

SECTION 2

The transportation or importation into any State, Territory, or Possession of the United States for delivery or use therein of intoxicating liquors, in violation of the laws thereof, is hereby prohibited.

Ratification

SECTION 3

This article shall be inoperative unless it shall have been ratified as an amendment to the Constitution by convention in the several States, as provided in the Constitution, within seven years from the date of the submission hereof to the States by the Congress.

This amendment repealed the Eighteenth Amendment, the Prohibition Amendment. It is the only amendment in our history which was ratified by state conventions, and the only amendment to be repealed in the long history of the Constitution.

With the advent of the 1929 depression, sentiment for the re-

peal of the Eighteenth Amendment increased. The banding together in the 1920's of the criminal elements associated with bootlegging and gang rule and gang wars led many people to question
the value of prohibition.

Repeal became an issue in the 1932 presidential campaign with
the Democratic Party in favor of outright repeal and the Republicans favoring resubmission of the amendment to the states. The
sweeping victory of the Democrats in the election resulted in the
passage of the repeal amendment by Congress on February 20,
1933. Utah was the thirty-seventh state to ratify on December 5,
1933. On the same day the President proclaimed the end of national prohibition.

Amendment XXII   PRESIDENTIAL   TENURE

Limitation of Terms

SECTION 1

*No person shall be elected to the office of the President more than
twice, and no person who has held the office of President, or acted as
President, for more than two years of a term to which some other
person was elected President shall be elected to the office of the President more than once. But this Article shall not apply to any person
holding the office of President when this Article was proposed by the
Congress, and shall not prevent any person who may be holding the
office of President, or acting as President, during the term within
which this Article becomes operative from holding the office of President or acting as President during the remainder of such term.*

Ratification

SECTION 2

*This Article shall be inoperative unless it shall have been ratified
as an amendment to the Constitution by the legislatures of three-
fourths of the several States within seven years from the date of its
submission to the States by the Congress.*

In the 160 years between 1787 and 1947, there were over 300
attempts by Congress to submit constitutional amendments changing presidential eligibility and tenure of office. All failed except

the proposal which has now become the Twenty-second Amendment to our Constitution.

George Washington established the two-term tradition in 1796 when he informed the country that he would retire as President at the conclusion of his second term. It was not broken until 1940 when Franklin D. Roosevelt was elected to a third term. He won a fourth term in 1944. Europe was in the throes of a total war in 1940, and in 1944 the United States was in the midst of a battle involving its very existence. These factors probably contributed to the breaking of the tradition. With the close of the war, agitation grew to re-establish the two-term tradition. When the Republicans gained control of Congress in the 1946 elections, one of their first actions was to submit a constitutional amendment limiting the President to two terms of four years each. The Twenty-second Amendment became effective on February 26, 1951.

Amendment XXIII PRESIDENTIAL ELECTORS FOR THE DISTRICT OF COLUMBIA

Number of Electors

SECTION 1

The District constituting the seat of Government of the United States shall appoint in such manner as the Congress may direct:

A number of electors of President and Vice President equal to the whole number of Senators and Representatives in Congress to which the District would be entitled if it were a State, but in no event more than the least populous State; they shall be in addition to those appointed by the States, but they shall be considered, for the purposes of the election of President and Vice President, to be electors appointed by a State; and they shall meet in the District and perform such duties as provided by the twelfth article of amendment.

Power of Congress

SECTION 2

The Congress shall have power to enforce this article by appropriate legislation.

On March 29, 1961, the Twenty-third Amendment was adopted by the State Legislature of Kansas, thereby completing the process of ratification. This amendment confers upon the citizens of the District of Columbia the right to vote for President and Vice President, a right lost by them since the Presidential election of 1800, when the District of Columbia was formed from the states of Maryland and Virginia. The District is given three electoral votes in each Presidential election.

A Developing Constitution

In the 169 years of history under the American Constitution, there have been nearly 5,000 constitutional amendments proposed to Congress. The twenty-three amendments we have just discussed and five other amendments which failed of ratification are all that have been submitted to the states. We have already noticed the first two of them, one providing for the reapportionment of Congress and the other setting forth a specific compensation for members of Congress. A third amendment was submitted in 1810 and forbade Americans to accept titles of nobility under any circumstances whatsoever. The fourth amendment was submitted in 1861 and provided specifically that the national government shall have no authority under any circumstances to interfere with the institution of Negro slavery. The fifth was submitted in 1924 and is known as the child-labor amendment.

A Flexible Constitution

Thus we see that the amending process of the Constitution has been used to bring about changes in it. It has given flexibility to the Constitution. Those who have argued that the process of amendment is too difficult have lost the force of their argument as a result of the adoption of the last eight amendments during the space of fifty years. The Sixteenth and Seventeenth Amendments became part of the Constitution in 1913, the Eighteenth and Nineteenth in 1920, the Twentieth and Twenty-first in 1933, the Twenty-second in 1951 and the Twenty-third in 1961.

Our Constitution is flexible not only through the process of amendment but also through the enactment of law by Congress. The framers laid down Congress' powers, and to Congress was left the duty of working out by law the means of exercising each power. In this way, law changes to meet changing conditions.

Washington once said that habit and time were the things that determined the true character of a government. Usage and custom have played an important part in our constitutional development. Our national political party system and our cabinet system are not provided for by the Constitution. They are examples of constitutional growth through usage and custom.

Judicial Interpretation

The greatest element of flexibility in our Constitution comes from the interpretation of the Constitution by the judiciary. Every section, clause, and line in the Constitution has come under the scrutiny of the courts. By hundreds of decisions, the Supreme Court has broadened and extended the powers of government. For example, when the commerce clause of the Constitution was written, the mode of travel was by stage coach, horseback, and sailing vessels. By court decision, the "commerce" clause has been broadened to include railroads, steamships, airplanes, radio, telegraph, and telephone. In the famous case of McCullough v. Maryland, the Supreme Court enunciated the doctrine of "implied powers." Although the Constitution did not specifically state that Congress had the power to charter a Bank of the United States, this court decision awarded Congress the power because it was thought "necessary and proper" in carrying out its specific powers to tax and provide revenue. Marshall wrote the doctrine of "implied powers" into American constitutional law with these words: "Let the end be legitimate, let it be within the scope of the Constitution, and all means which are appropriate, which are plainly adopted to that end, and which are not prohibited but consistent with the letter and spirit of the Constitution, are constitutional."

In other words, the Supreme Court (and the American people) now apparently accepts the thesis that Congress can do anything which it may deem necessary in exercising a power as long as it does not directly violate the Constitution. Many other cases could be cited to show how the Constitution expands by court interpretation, but this suffices to emphasize the importance of judicial interpretation under our system of government.

By the amending process, by development of law, by custom and usage, and by judicial interpretation, the Constitution is a living instrument, always adjustable to a changing society.

Struck from the pens of those immortal Americans who sat in the Constitutional Conventions in less than 5,000 words (hardly more than the length of a school term paper), the Constitution of the United States remains the greatest document of free government ever devised by mankind.

TOPICAL OUTLINE FOR STUDY

A. Eleventh Amendment
B. Twelfth Amendment
C. Thirteenth Amendment
D. Fourteenth Amendment
  1. American citizenship
  2. Privileges and immunities of citizens of the United States
  3. Life, liberty, and property safeguarded from the state
  4. Equal protection of the laws
  5. Representation
  6. Exclusion of Confederates from Federal office
  7. Repudiation of Confederate debt
E. Fifteenth Amendment
F. Sixteenth Amendment
G. Seventeenth Amendment
H. Eighteenth Amendment
I. Nineteenth Amendment
J. Twentieth Amendment
K. Twenty-first Amendment
L. Twenty-second Amendment
M. Twenty-third Amendment

QUESTIONS

1. What is the historical significance of Chisholm v. Georgia?
2. What defect existed in the original provisions of the Constitution dealing with the election of the President and Vice President? How was it corrected?
3. What does the Thirteenth Amendment provide?

4. What effect did the Fourteenth Amendment have on citizenship?
5. What portions of the Constitution did the Fourteenth Amendment supersede?
6. How did the Fourteenth Amendment deal with the confederates?
7. What is the most important section of the Fourteenth Amendment?
8. Does the Fifteenth Amendment confer the right to vote on anyone?
9. What was the significance of:
   (a) Springer v. United States
   (b) Pollock v. Farmers' Loan and Trust Company?
10. What did the Sixteenth Amendment provide?
11. Why was the Seventeenth Amendment added to the Constitution?
12. Explain the provisions of the Seventeenth Amendment.
13. What was the most famous Constitutional amendment in American history?
14. What is the only Constitutional amendment in our history which was ratified by state ratifying conventions?
15. What does the Nineteenth Amendment provide?
16. What did the Twentieth Amendment do to
   (a) "Lame duck" Congresses
   (b) Inauguration date
   (c) Terms of President and Vice President
   (d) Date for Congress to assemble
   (e) Succession to the presidency?
17. What does the Twenty-first Amendment provide?
18. What did the Twenty-second Amendment do to presidential tenure?
19. What five amendments have been submitted to the states for ratification but have thus far failed of ratification?
20. Why has the "amending process" given flexibility to the Constitution?
21. Have the twenty-three amendments to the Constitution changed any of the major principles of the Constitution?
22. How does Congress make the Constitution flexible by enactment of laws?
23. How has the Constitution grown through custom and usage?
24. What is the greatest element of flexibility in the Constitution?
25. By what processes does the Constitution adjust itself to ever-changing society?
26. What does the Twenty-second Amendment provide?

Selected Bibliography

ANDERSON, WILLIAM: *The Nation and the States, Rivals or Partners?* University of Minnesota Press, Minneapolis, 1955.

BEARD, CHARLES A.: *The Enduring Federalist.* Doubleday and Company, Inc., New York, 1948.

BERNSTEIN, M. H.: *The Job of the Federal Executive.* Brookings Institution, Washington, D. C., 1958.

BLOOM, SOL: *The Story of the Constitution.* The United States Constitution, Sesquicentennial Commission, Government Printing Office, Washington, D. C., 1937.

BLOOM, SOL: *History of the Formation of the Union under the Constitution.* United States Government Printing Office, Washington, D. C., 1941.

CHAFEE, ZECHARIAH, JR.: *Free Speech in the United States.* Harvard University Press, Cambridge, 1948.

CORWIN, EDWARD: *The President—Office and Powers.* New York University Press, New York, Revised Edition.

CORWIN, E. S.: *Total War and the Constitution.* Alfred A. Knopf, New York, 1947.

CORWIN AND KOENIG: *The Presidency Today.* New York University Press, New York, 1956.

COUSINS, NORMAN: *In God We Trust.* Harper and Brothers, New York, 1958.

HAND, LEARNED: *The Bill of Rights.* Harvard University Press, Cambridge, 1958.

HART, JAMES: *The American Presidency in Action—1789.* Macmillan Company, New York, 1948.

HOLCOMBE, ARTHUR N.: *Our More Perfect Union.* Harvard University Press, Cambridge, 1950.

JENSEN, MERRILL: *The New Nation—A History of the United States During the Confederation.* Alfred A. Knopf, New York, 1950.

LOTH, DAVID: *Chief Justice John Marshall and the Growth of the Republic.* W. W. Norton Company, New York, 1949.

MADISON, JAMES: *Journal of the Constitutional Convention.* Scott, Foresman and Company, Chicago, 1896.

MORLEY, FELIX: *The Power in the People.* D. Van Nostrand Company, Inc., New York, 1949.

PATTERSON, BENNETT B.: *The Forgotten Ninth Amendment.* Bobbs-Merrill Company, Indianapolis, 1955.

ROSSITER, CLINTON: *The Supreme Court and the Commander in Chief.* Cornell University Press, New York, 1951.

ROSSITER, CLINTON: *The American Presidency.* Harcourt, Brace and Company, New York, 1956.

SCHUBERT, GLENDON A., JR.: *The Presidency in the Courts.* University of Minnesota Press, Minneapolis, 1957.

STEVENS, C. E.: *Sources of the Constitution of the United States.* Macmillan Company, New York, 1927.

Swisher, Carl Brent: *The Growth of Constitutional Power in the United States.* University of Chicago Press, Chicago, 1946.
Swisher, Carl Brent: *American Constitutional Development.* Houghton Mifflin Company, New York, 1943.
Wilmerding, Lucius: *The Electoral College.* Rutgers University Press, New Brunswick, 1958.
Van Doren, Carl: *The Great Rehearsal.* Viking Press, Inc., New York, 1948.
Vreeland, Hamilton: *Twilight of Individual Liberty.* Scribner's (Charles) Sons, New York, 1944.
Congressional Quarterly Weekly Report
U. S. News and World Report

Index to the Constitution

Subject Index